Rosalind M. and Jac. J. Janssen

Growing up
in Ancient Egypt

 The Rubicon Press

The Rubicon Press
57 Cornwall Gardens
London SW7 4BE

First printed 1990
Reprinted 1996

British Library Cataloguing in Publication Data

ISBN 0-948695-15-3 (hbk)
ISBN 0-948695-16-1 (pbk)

Designed and typeset by The Rubicon Press
Printed and bound in Great Britain by Biddles Limited of Guildford
and King's Lynn

Contents

List of Illustrations

13. Ay and his wife Teye rewarded by the royal family. From the tomb of Ay at el-Amarna, Eighteenth Dynasty (After Davies, *The Rock Tombs of El Amarna*, VI, 1908, plate XXIX).

14. Child's pleated linen dress. From mastaba 2050 at Tarkhan, First Dynasty (UC 28614B[1]. Courtesy of the Petrie Museum of Egyptian Archaeology, University College London).

15. A pair of child's linen sleeves. From tomb 25 at Gurob, late Eighteenth to early Nineteenth Dynasty (UC 8980 A and B. Courtesy of the Petrie Museum of Egyptian Archaeology, University College London).

16. Girl wearing a fish-shaped pendant. From the tomb of Ukhhotep (C1) at Meir, Twelfth Dynasty (After Blackman and Apted, *The Rock Tombs of Meir*, VI, 1953, plate XIV).

17. Children's jewellery: (a) electrum side-lock pendant. Unprovenanced, Middle Kingdom. Both sides, scale 1:1 (Fitzwilliam Museum Cambridge EGA 155.1947); (b) gold catfish hair ornament. From tomb 72 at Haraga, Twelfth Dynasty. Scale 1:1 (Royal Museum of Scotland, Edinburgh 1914.1079).

18. Nefer, with his pet dog, accompanied by his nude daughter who clutches a lapwing. From the mastaba of Nefer at Saqqara, Fifth Dynasty (After Moussa and Altenmüller, *The Tomb of Nefer and Ka-Hay*, 1971, plate 2).

19. Children's toys: (above) left and right, painted reed and linen balls. Unprovenanced, Roman Period; (centre) blue faience tops. From the Faiyum, Roman Period; (below) wooden feline with crystal eyes and a moveable jaw fitted with bronze teeth. From Thebes, New Kingdom (EA 46709-10; 34920-21; 15671. Courtesy of the Trustees of the British Museum).

20. Painted wooden doll with moveable arms. She originally had a wig of mud beads. From tomb 58 at Hawara, Twelfth Dynasty (UC 16148. Courtesy of the Petrie Museum of Egyptian Archaeology, University College London).

21. In a kitchen hut one man is at work while his companion, who is eating, orders a boy to run an errand. The hieroglyphs give the lad's answer: "I'll do it". From the tomb of Pepiankh (A2) at Meir, Twelfth Dynasty (After Blackman and Apted, *The Rock Tombs of Meir*, V, 1953, plate XXX).

22. A boy and a girl threatened by an irate doorkeeper while their nanny drinks from a jar. Part of a scene in which a lady is received by the Pharaoh Ay in the palace gardens. From the Theban tomb of Neferhotep (TT 49), Eighteenth Dynasty (After Davies, *The Tomb of Nefer-hotep at Thebes*, I, 1931, plate XIV).

23. Boys' games: (a) star game; (b) balancing act. From the mastaba of Ptahhotep at Saqqara, Fifth Dynasty (After Touny and Wenig, *Der Sport im Alten Ägypten*, 1969, figure 32).

24. Boys' games: (a) *khazza lawizza*; (b) ?stampers. From the mastaba of Ptahhotep at Saqqara, Fifth Dynasty (After Touny and Wenig, *Der Sport im Alten Ägypten*, 1969, figure 34).

25. Painted limestone group statuette of a boy and a girl playing. From the tomb of Ny-kau-inpu at Giza, Fifth to Sixth Dynasty (OI 10639. Courtesy of the Oriental Institute of the University of Chicago).

26. Painted limestone ostracon showing a mouse juggling with two balls. From Deir el-Medina, New Kingdom (MM 14 048. Courtesy of the Medelhavsmuseet, Stockholm).

27. Painted limestone relief: (centre register) left, a fertility dance; right, the 'hut game'. From ?Giza, late Fifth to early Sixth Dynasty (After James, *Hieroglyphic Texts from Egyptian Stelae, etc.*, I, 2nd ed., 1961, plate XXV; now British Museum EA 994).

28. Black granite statue of an anonymous high official in the attitude of a scribe. From Saqqara, Fifth Dynasty (AST 31. Courtesy of the Rijksmuseum van Oudheden, Leiden).

29. Limestone block statue of the High Priest of Amun Bekenkhons inscribed with an autobiographical text. From Thebes, Nineteenth Dynasty (G1. WAF 38. Courtesy of the Staatliche Sammlung Ägyptischer Kunst, Munich).

30. Pierced limestone schoolboy's writing board with six horizontal lines of hieratic text comprising a letter exchanged between two scribes exhorting the scribal profession. From Abydos, Twentieth Dynasty (E. 580. Courtesy of the Musées Royaux d'Art et d'Histoire, Brussels).

31. A high official followed by his apprentice son who carries a papyrus roll and a writing tablet. From the Theban tomb of Djeserkareseneb (TT 38), Eighteenth Dynasty (After Davies, *Scenes from Some Theban Tombs*, 1963, plate II).

32. The wife of a mayor of Thebes seated beside her husband, with a palette and a scribal kit bag below her chair. From the Theban tomb of Kenamun (TT 162), Eighteenth Dynasty (After Davies, *Scenes from Some Theban Tombs*, 1963, plate XVI).

33. Limestone ostracon with the names of Amenophis I in cartouches, placed over the hieroglyphic sign for gold. (a) The recto written by the master; (b) the verso copied by a pupil. From Deir el-Medina, New Kingdom (MM 14 116. Courtesy of the Medelhavsmuseet, Stockholm).

34. Pottery ostracon inscribed in black ink with practice drawings of standard figures by a sculptor's pupil. From Deir el-Medina, New Kingdom (After Page, *Ancient Egyptian Figured Ostraca*, 1983, Cat. No. 81; now UC 33241).

35. Circumcision scene: right, the preparation; left, the operation itself. From the mastaba of Ankhmahor at Saqqara, Sixth Dynasty (After Badawy, *The Tomb of Nyhetep-Ptah at Giza and the Tomb of 'Ankh-m'ahor at Saqqara*, 1978, figure 27).

36. Circumcision of the Divine King and his *ka*. From the "Birth Chamber" of the Luxor Temple, Eighteenth Dynasty (After Brunner, *Die Geburt des Gottkönigs*, 1964, plate 15).

37. Wooden statue of Meryrehashtef as a young adult, clearly showing circumcision. From tomb 274 at Sedment, Sixth Dynasty (ÆIN 1560. Courtesy of the Ny Carlsberg Glyptotek, Copenhagen).

38. The conscription of recruits for the army. From the Theban tomb of Tjanuny (TT 74), Eighteenth Dynasty (After Champollion, *Monuments*, II, 1845, plate CLVII).

39. Painted limestone statue of Ra-maat wearing the gala-kilt with knotted girdle. From Giza, early Sixth Dynasty (PM 420. Courtesy of the Roemer-Pelizaeus Museum, Hildesheim).

40. A bride at her wedding celebrations. From Western Thebes, 1989 (Courtesy of Mr. John Mellors).
41. Limestone stela of Paneb who (above) adores a coiled serpent, doubtless Mertseger, the goddess of the Theban necropolis; (below) three of his descendants, including (right) his son Opakhte. From Deir el-Medina, Nineteenth Dynasty (EA 272. Courtesy of the Trustees of the British Museum).
42. Figure of Khaemwese in its naos. Unprovenanced. Now lost, but in the early eighteenth century A.D. housed in a private collection in London (From Gordon, *An Essay Towards Explaining the Hieroglyphical Figures on the Coffin of the Ancient Mummy Belonging to Capt. William Lethieullier*, 1737, plate V).
43. Kenamun's mother Amenemopet nurses Amenophis II. From the Theban tomb of Kenamun (TT 93), Eighteenth Dynasty (After Davies, *The Tomb of Ken-Amūn at Thebes*, 1930, plate IX).
44. Paheri with his pupil Prince Wadzmose on his lap. From the tomb of Paheri at el-Kab, Eighteenth Dynasty (After Tylor and Griffith, *The Tomb of Paheri at El Kab*, 1894, plate IV).
45. Black granite statue of Senenmut holding the Princess Neferure. She wears a false beard equating her with the young Theban god Khonsu. From Thebes, Eighteenth Dynasty (EA 174. Courtesy of the Trustees of the British Museum).
46. Hekareshu with four princes on his lap. From Theban tomb 226, Eighteenth Dynasty (After Davies, *The Tombs of Menkheperrasonb, Amenmosĕ, and Another*, 1933, plate XXX).
47. The sportive king: (a) Min gives an archery lesson to Prince Amenophis. From the Theban tomb of Min (TT 109), Eighteenth Dynasty (After Davies, *BMMA* Nov. 1935, figure 7); (b) Red granite block showing Amenophis II shooting at a copper target. From Karnak, Eighteenth Dynasty (After Bothmer, *The Luxor Museum Catalogue*, 1979, figure 53; now Luxor Museum J.129).
48. Wrestling and single-stick fighting: (a) From the First Court of the Medinet Habu Temple, Twentieth Dynasty (After *Medinet Habu* II = *Later Historical Records of Ramesses III*, 1932, plate 111); (b) At Abydos, A.D. 1901 (Photograph by Margaret Murray. Courtesy of the Petrie Museum of Egyptian Archaeology, University College London).
49. Ramesses III chucks his daughter under her chin. From the Eastern High Gate of the Medinet Habu Temple, Twentieth Dynasty (After *Medinet Habu* VIII = *The Eastern High Gate*, 1970, plate 639).
50. White sandstone stela of the Viceroy Usersatet. From the second cataract fortress of Semna, Eighteenth Dynasty (MFA 25.632. Courtesy of the Museum of Fine Arts, Boston).
51. Grey granite and limestone colossal statue of Ramesses II with the falcon god Hurun. From Tanis, Nineteenth Dynasty (JE 64735. Courtesy of the Egyptian Museum, Cairo).
52. Opaque red moulded glass inlay showing two young Amarna princesses. From el-Amarna, Eighteenth Dynasty (UC 2235. Courtesy of the Petrie Museum of Egyptian Archaeology, University College London).
53. Map of Egypt, showing the sites mentioned in the text and the captions.

Acknowledgements

We wish to express our gratitude to the many museum curators and the one private individual who have provided photographs, in many cases gratis, and permission for their publication. Each institution is fully credited in the List of Illustrations. Mr. Peter Harrison and his staff of the Central Photographic Unit, University College London, deserve the highest praise for the habitual skill with which they have produced our other photographs. The line drawings are the painstaking work of Juanita Homan.

Visits to the Museum of Childhood at Bethnal Green, London, were a source of joy and inspiration to us.

To Anthea Page and Juanita Homan, the Editors of The Rubicon Press, we express our sincere thanks for their ever willing help, lively interest, and continuous encouragement.

Finally, it is not usual to thank one's co-author, especially when that person happens to be a spouse, for stimulation and support. But in view of the fact that this book came to be written during our first year of marriage, perhaps it is not so very surprising that we should wish to do so!

Preface

The title of this book is borrowed from Hamed Ammar's classic study *Growing up in an Egyptian Village* (London, 1954). Whereas he, however, originated from the village which he describes (namely Silwa, midway between Kom Ombo and Edfu) and could base his account on his own memories as well as on lengthy discussions with his informants from that community, we were wholly dependent upon written sources and objects that have by chance survived. Moreover, whereas his aim was sociological and educational, ours was purely historical. We did not search for general theories, instead we wanted to understand one individual case: the Ancient Egyptian civilization from a particular aspect, that of the child and childhood.

So far as we are aware this is the first book on the subject. Of course, there exist many articles, and even some more extensive studies, on specific features of the younger generation in Ancient Egypt, but no general book of this kind seems ever to have appeared. The only scholarly work we know of is the Habilitationsschrift of Professor Erika Feucht of the University of Heidelberg, but, unfortunately, this has not yet been published. Professor Feucht kindly sent us some recent articles, in which she has summarized particular aspects of her study, and more can be found in the lemma 'Kind' in the *Lexikon der Ägyptologie* (vol. III, col. 424-437, with no less than 169 notes). For her generous help we are exceedingly grateful.

Other literature on which we have based our text is quoted in the bibliography, but numerous details are derived from everywhere in the Egyptological output. Our colleagues will easily recognize most of them; for the general reader, for whom this book is intended, they are too specific to be of interest.

As regards the translations from Egyptian texts, scholars will immediately see that many are taken from those three invaluable volumes of Miriam Lichtheim, *Ancient Egyptian Literature* (Berkeley, 1973-1980), although with slight alterations where they seemed necessary for our purpose. The sources for other quotations are generally familiar to every Egyptologist. We have throughout adapted them to the style of our book, avoiding as far as possible the specific "translator's language" found in scientific studies.

In our choice of illustrations we have attempted to steer clear of pictures and objects that are common in popular works on Ancient Egypt. In some chapters that was easy, the material being abundant; in others we could not completely escape from the well-known. Yet, all our photographs and line drawings were chosen because they illustrate some part of the text, even where the objects or representations were in themselves far from aesthetically pleasing.

Of course, we hope that the reader will enjoy this not so common study on a particular aspect of Egyptian civilization, and that he or she will thereby broaden his/her knowledge. We suspect that no one, however, will learn as much from it as we ourselves have. This means that writing this book, although 'work' to us, at no time threatened to become a chore, and was mostly a pastime of the utmost satisfaction.

February 1990   Rosalind and Jac. Janssen

I Pregnancy and Birth

Both myths and stories from Ancient Egypt reveal some bizarre ideas about conception. The sky goddess Nut, for instance, was believed to swallow the sun every evening at dusk in order to give birth to it anew every dawn morning. In the New Kingdom *Story of the Two Brothers* the hero Bata is transformed into a tree. When this tree is felled at the request of the Queen, Bata's ex-wife, a splinter flies into her mouth. She immediately becomes pregnant and, many days later, she gives birth to a son. Yet, such miraculous narratives do not reflect the everyday notions of the Egyptians, no more than that the Greeks really believed a child could be born from its father's head, as Athena was from Zeus.

More realistic remarks are contained in other stories. For example, in the New Kingdom composition *Truth and Falsehood* a lady espies a blind tramp who had been found under a thicket, and she desires him since he is handsome. "He slept with her that night, and knew her with the knowledge of a man, and she conceived a son that night". In the contemporary *Tale of the Doomed Prince* there occurs a king who has no son. He begs one from the gods, and they decree that an heir should be born to him. "That night he slept with his wife, and she [became] pregnant. When she had completed the months of childbearing, a son was born".

That rational beliefs regarding conception were in vogue appears evident from medical papyri (fig. 1). Written in hieratic (cursive) script, these contain advice on ways to stimulate it, as well as indicating methods of birth control, albeit without using any kind of contraceptive aid. Unwanted pregnancy was obviously now unknown, for there are prescriptions to stimulate an abortion, together with those designed to prevent the occurrence of a miscarriage, which include the use of a tampon as occasionally depicted on the oil vessels described below. To modern eyes some of these procedures are hardly practical, and great reliance is placed

1

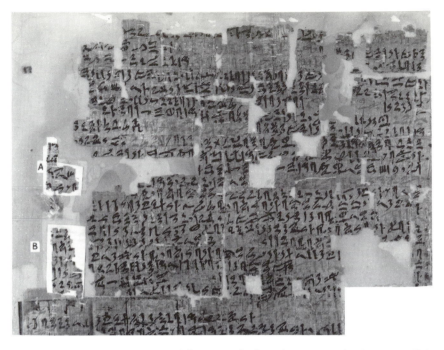

Gynaecological papyrus containing prescriptions for women (Kahun, Twelfth Dynasty). (Fig. 1)

on purely magical spells, but the texts do show that the physical process was known, although not of course in all biological details.

These papyri also indicate the means to establish whether a woman is pregnant, some of which are indeed quite sound. For instance, taking her pulse, observing the colour of both her skin and eyes, and testing her propensity to vomit, just three logical signs. However, much more irrational, but obviously typical, magical practices were adopted in order to discern pregnancy and the sex of the unborn child:

> You shall put wheat and barley into purses of cloth.
> The woman shall pass her water on it, every day.
> If both sprout, she will bear.
> If the wheat sprouts, she will bear a boy.
> If the barley sprouts, she will bear a girl.
> If neither sprouts, she will not bear at all.

A second similar example reads: "A crushed plant is mixed with milk of a woman who has given birth to a boy. If another woman drinks it and vomits, she will give birth; if she emits wind, she will never give birth".

How pregnancy became news is told in the Demotic *Story of Setne*, of the Graeco-Roman era. A woman, who after conceiving reached her appointed time of cleaning, underwent no purification. When women purified themselves after menstruation, it was evidently publicly known, so that "it was reported to the Pharaoh and his heart was very happy".

Pregnant women, as is still the case today, were accustomed to massage themselves with oil in order to prevent stretch marks and to ease the birth itself, if they could afford it with a valuable perfumed brand. In the Eighteenth Dynasty this liquid was sometimes stored in special anthropomorphous containers taking the form of a naked, childbearing figure, either standing or squatting (fig. 3). She rubs her abdomen with both hands and exhibits a distinct lack of genitalia, occasionally with a prominent tampon to prevent either miscarriage or to check the escape of blood at the birth.

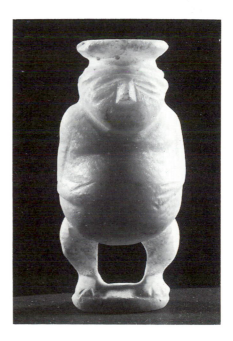

Calcite oil vessel in the shape of a standing pregnant woman with grotesque features. H. 8.5 cm. (Unprovenanced, Eighteenth Dynasty). (Fig. 3)

Their grotesque faces and pendulous breasts show obvious affinities to Thoeris the pregnant hippopotamus goddess (fig. 2b). In one instance she holds an oil-horn, illustrating the intended contents of these vessels. The particular shape of the small vases, normally made of calcite (Egyptian alabaster), was believed to possess an additional magical force. Examples were even exported to Crete and Syro-Palestine.

The duration of pregnancy was of course roughly familiar from experience, as evidenced by the phrase "when she had completed the months of childbearing", already quoted above from the *Tale of the Doomed Prince*. However, nowhere are the nine months explicitly mentioned, the nearest proof being the sentence in the New Kingdom *Instruction of Any*: "when you were born after *your* months". In a folktale from the Middle Kingdom composition known as the *Tales of Wonder* (Papyrus Westcar) the king asks a magician, Djedi, when a woman will give birth. The answer is: on the fifteenth day of the fifth month of the year. However, although Djedi was old, wise and respected, we must remember that this is a fairy tale!

Delivery took place in special surroundings, namely in a distinctive structure known as the confinement pavilion, or else in a particular room of the house. The former is depicted in New Kingdom wall paintings in the houses of the artisans of Deir el-Medina at Western Thebes, and in those of the workmen's village East of el-Amarna. The documentation is necessarily scanty since hardly any houses of common folk have been preserved elsewhere, and most murals have anyway been largely destroyed.

However, figured ostraca (broken pottery sherds or flakes of limestone) from Deir el-Medina, clearly copies of and/or models for these paintings, present a fairly reliable picture. They show (fig. 4) a pavilion with papyrus stalks forming the columns which are decorated with tendrils of the convolvulus or grapevine. Sometimes garlands are hung on the walls. Clearly specifically erected, immediately prior to the confinement, in the garden or on the roof, its walls consist of plants and its roof is a mat.

Such a structure seems to be pictured in one of the rooms of the royal tomb at el-Amarna, which is situated deep in the desert, in a wadi East of the city. However, Princess Meketaten is here

4

Painted limestone ostracon depicting the confinement pavilion. A servant girl offers a mirror and a kohl tube to a lying-in woman suckling her child (Deir el-Medina, New Kingdom). (Fig. 4)

represented standing in the pavilion, while Akhenaten and Nefertiti, and three of the princesses, are depicted in the habitual attitude of mourning. Clearly the Pharaoh's second daughter had died in childbirth, as is confirmed by another scene in the same room. There she is lying on a bier; her parents are again portrayed in the posture of mourning, while a nurse carries an evidently living baby from the room. That this was a royal child is indicated by the women following the nurse, for they bear fans, the sign of royalty. The death-room of Meketaten is badly mutilated, but seems to have been unadorned, hence it is not a representation of the birth chamber.

In daily life, so far as less wealthy people were concerned, confinement would have taken place in a normal room in the house, the decoration being the wall paintings mentioned above. These particularly depict two divinities: the dwarf god Bes (fig. 2a), connected with sexuality and fertility, and Thoeris, the patroness of pregnant women, once called "she who removes the (birth) waters". At Deir el-Medina the low walls of a kind of platform can still be seen in the front room, on which the birth took place, as the remaining decoration corroborates.

Particular furniture is shown in the pavilion, comprising a bed with a mattress, a headrest, a mat and a cushion, and a stool fashioned from a palm-tree stump. Toilet equipment, such as a mirror, is also illustrated. Apotropaeic wands (see below) and the special confinement stool of today, with its wide opening in the seat, are not depicted. On most occasions, as is still the practice in primitive societies, birth would have taken place when the woman was squatting on some bricks. There is a spell which is spoken over such confinement bricks. Actually it is a hymn to Meskhenet (fig. 2d), the personification of the confinement chair, portrayed in human guise with the uterus of a cow on her head. The spell derives from a hymn to the goddess of heaven.

The woman was assisted during her labour by some elderly female relatives, one grasping her from behind, one kneeling before her. It is doubtful whether trained midwives existed. In the *Tales of Wonder*, as we shall see, the function is performed by itinerant dancing girls. It has been suggested that the profession was 'impure' and hence not highly esteemed. In the texts from Deir el-Medina 'wise women' feature, but, so far as we know, they merely practiced divination. There is no indication that the husband was present at the birth, and the special pavilion indeed points to separation.

6

On the other hand, a front room, through which everyone had to enter or leave the house, made isolation problematic.

In all representations of either this confinement pavilion or of the birth chamber the mother is shown practically naked, sitting on the bed or the stool while suckling her baby. She wears only a collar and a girdle, and her headdress is conspicuous. It consists of bunches of hair standing out on both sides of the head, and a cone bound by a piece of cord on its crown. It has been surmised that the hair of a woman in labour was initially tightly bound and later loosened in order, by sympathetic magic, to accelerate birth. It is from this hair-style that we can recognize the lying-in woman and the young mother.

This type of hair-style also occurs on the so-called 'concubine' figures of the New Kingdom, although the majority exhibit a full festal wig (fig. 5). The objects, made of terracotta or limestone, portray a naked woman lying either on a bed or on a plank, sometimes with a child, usually male, beside her thigh or being suckled. They have been interpreted as 'erotic' (which they certainly are), bedmates of a deceased man. In fact, they were intended to stimulate fertility in all aspects, with the precise aim also of projecting the image of mother and child. The fact that they occur in burials points to the continuation of these functions in the netherworld. This interpretation is reinforced by a particular Middle Kingdom female figure in East Berlin. The free-standing form carries a child on her left hip and exhibits an inscription on the opposite leg, which reads: "May there be given birth to your daughter Sah". The model was put into the tomb of the father. To prevent escape from this funerary context, the birds among the hieroglyphs miss their legs, as does the woman herself. Although not lying on a bed, this object too - not the only example of this type - clearly belongs to the category of fertility figures.

In the pictures of the birth pavilion the mother is attended by girls who are as naked as she and sport the same hair-style. In a few instances a Nubian boy is shown with equally conspicuous hair: shaved and with a prominent tuft on the crown (see p. 40). This personnel assists the lady at her toilet and waits upon her with food and drink. Perhaps the representation depicts the ritual and accompanying feast at the end of the isolation period (of four-

Painted limestone concubine figure lying on a bed. Convolvulus decoration at each side and infant at bottom right (Gurob, Nineteenth Dynasty). (Fig. 5)

teen days; see the *Tales of Wonder* below). Based on this scene there are also satirical drawings on ostraca where the mother is a mouse and the servants cats. In both cases the attendants are clearly dressing their mistress for her re-entrance into the world.

8

Birth is a dangerous event, and was nowhere more so regarded than in the ancient world. Therefore, it was surrounded by an aura of magical superstition. In one spell a dwarf (clearly Bes) is summoned, who is sent by the sun-god Re. The recitation runs:

> Come down, placenta, come down, come down! I am Horus who
> conjures in order that she who is giving birth becomes better than she was, as if she was already delivered . . . . . Look, Hathor will lay her hand on her with an amulet of health! I am Horus who saves her!

This has to be recited four times, probably by the 'midwife', over a dwarf of clay (an amulet in the form of Bes) placed on the brow of a woman who is undergoing a difficult labour.

A particular magical artefact connected with pregnancy and the baby, and already mentioned in passing above, is the so-called apotropaeic wand (fig. 6). It was formerly referred to as a magical knife, although it possesses no sharp edge. In appearance it looks like a boomerang, the sickle-shape being due to the fact that it is made of hippopotamus teeth. However, some of these objects are made of calcite, faience, or ebony. A total of about a hundred and fifty surviving examples are known, all dating from the Middle Kingdom and the Second Intermediate Period.

They have a flat and a convex face, on both of which are incised rows of demons: griffins, snake-headed cheetahs, the divinities Bes and Thoeris, and figures referring to the sun-god such as a seated cat or a double lion. In several instances the flat side also bears an inscription, for example the phrase: "protection by night and day", or a more extensive formula: "words spoken by these protective figures: we have come to spread protection over this child". Then follows the name of the juvenile, always a boy, or that of a woman, evidently the mother.

These items would have been used in a ritual, and were probably laid either on the stomach of a pregnant woman or on the body of the baby. Their function was to identify the infant with the sun-god Re, who was threatened in his youth by such monsters. As he survived, so by inference will the new-born child be safe. In

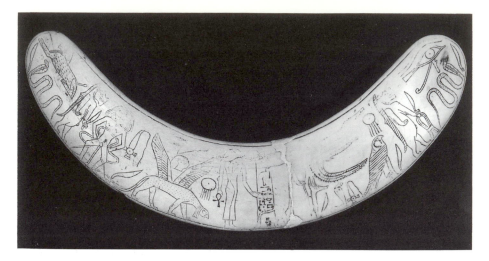

Hippopotamus ivory apotropaeic wand inscribed for the "Lady of the House Seneb". L. 37 cm. (Thebes, Twelfth Dynasty). (Fig. 6)

one instance, namely in the tomb of the nomarch (provincial governor) Dhutihotep at el-Bersheh in Middle Egypt, the wand occurs in the hand of what seems to be a nanny or wet-nurse, confirming that it was used around the event of the birth of a child.

Another proof that magical practices were customary is the discovery, in a cupboard beneath the stairs of a house at el-Amarna, of four objects. They comprised a small painted limestone stela (upright slab) depicting a woman and a girl adoring Thoeris; a terracotta figure of a naked female with the typical hair-style of the lying-in woman and very prominent breasts; and two painted pottery beds. It can be suggested that these items were used at the confinement, and subsequently stored safely away, perhaps for future occasions. All four clearly refer to fertility and childbirth.

Above we cited the *Tales of Wonder*, a compilation of folk stories. In one of them the Pharaoh, the famous Khufu (Cheops) of the Fourth Dynasty, hears about an old and wise magician named Djedi. This sage is brought to the court by a prince, for the king hopes that he can reveal to him the place where a secret is hidden. Indeed Djedi says he does know it, but it would only be found by "the eldest of the three children who are in the womb of Ruddedet". Then Djedi tells the king, as quoted above, when the triplets will be born.

10

In the continuation of the story the delivery of the woman is recounted: "On one of these days Ruddedet felt the pangs and her labour was difficult. Then the Majesty of Re, Lord of Sabkhu (a Delta town), said to Isis, Nephthys, Meskhenet, Heqet (a frog-headed goddess of birth; fig. 2c), and Khnum (the ram-headed god of Elephantine): 'Please go and deliver Ruddedet of the three children who are in her womb, who will assume this beneficient office in the land'"; that is, who in future will become Pharaohs.

The four goddesses go, with Khnum as their porter, disguised as dancing girls. When they reach the house they find Ruddedet's husband, the priest Ranofer, standing before it in distress, for the throes are painful. The ladies claim to have the knowledge of mid-wives and are requested to enter. Isis places herself before the woman, Nephthys behind her (as described above), while Heqet hastens the birth. When the child appears Isis pronounces the name of the boy, and he "slid into her arms, one cubit long, strong in bones, his limbs overlaid with gold, his headdress of true lapis lazuli". Clearly he shows all the markings of a royal child. The goddesses wash the baby after first having cut the umbilical cord, and lay it on a pillow of cloth. The same happens with the two other boys.

Afterwards the ladies with their servant vacate the house, leaving behind in a sealed room the sack of barley they had received as their recompense. Secretly they had placed three crowns of gold in the sack. Then "Ruddedet cleansed herself in a cleansing of fourteen days", the time the young mother had to spend in isolation in the confinement chamber or pavilion. The miracles that follow concerning the crowns are of no importance to us here.

Although a tale and full of supernatural events, the narrative evidently contains references to daily life, and is, therefore, the only written source we possess about birth. Some elements are missing, especially the confinement stool; others are only clear from this particular text, such as the role of the 'midwives' and their lowly status in society. But undoubtedly the story presents a picture of reality.

One further subject merits discussion. In the tale just related triplets are born, a relatively rare matter, mentioned nowhere else in Egyptian sources. Twins, however, were certainly less unusual.

11

Approximately one per cent of all births must have resulted in twins, over half of them like-sexed. In view of the high infant mortality rate only a total of 0.3 per cent would have survived. Yet during the millennia of Egyptian history this presupposes a considerable number.

Curiously enough, only three pairs are at present known. One of them, the brothers Niankhkhnum and Khnumhotep, of the Fifth Dynasty, shared an impressive tomb at Saqqara. On its walls they are represented holding hands and even embracing - which is generally only seen in couples -, expressing their close relationship. Niankhkhnum as the eldest twin is accorded a slight superiority in his position in the scenes. They occupied the same post, that of manicurist to the king, which means that they belonged to the inner court circles. Moreover, they were administrators of the royal properties, which explains the wealth of their burial.

The second pair are the architects of the Amun Temple under Amenophis III, Suti and Hor, well-known from their grey granite stela inscribed with a hymn to Aten (the god of the 'heretic' Pharaoh Akhenaten), now in the British Museum. That they were indeed twins is evident from a sentence in this text: "He (my brother) went forth with me from the womb on the same day". They were named after the gods Seth and Horus who, according to the myths, were uncle and nephew. However, the Egyptian word for 'brother' encompasses the relationships of brother, cousin, nephew and uncle.

A third pair may be the two sisters represented on a Twelfth Dynasty stela, now in Paris. They are also shown embracing, and both are called "his (the owner of the stela) beloved daughter Sitamun".

Three instances are certainly not very many, but in later times there is more evidence. We then find a special word for twins, and 'twin' even developed into a common name (in Greek 'Didymos'). Yet, the documentation for the flowering epochs of Egyptian history is conspicuously meagre. There is, for instance, no evidence for unlike-sexed twins.

One explanation could be that, as in other cultures, twins were killed, either one of them or both; but it must be emphasized that there is not a shred of proof for this. It has also been suggested that multiple births, regarded as weird, an accident or even a misfortune, excluded the children from public life; or that it was ignored in the texts so that we never hear about them. On the other hand, Niankhkhnum and Khnumhotep were closely connected to the king, and Suty and Hor received divine names. That suggests that twins were rather conceived of as an anomaly in the world-order, honoured but requiring symbolic correction in order to be acceptable. They seem to have been regarded as an incompletely formed unity, or an excess of unity, in either case contradicting concord.

Obviously this particular facet of Egyptian civilization requires further study, as indeed do other aspects of the fascinating sphere of pregnancy and birth.

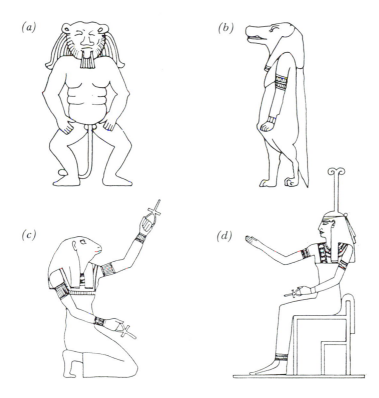

Four divinities connected with birth: (a) Bes; (b) Thoeris; (c) Heqet; (d) Meskhenet (Deir el-Bahri, Eighteenth Dynasty). (Fig. 2)

13

II   The Baby

As we have already seen from the *Tales of Wonder*, the child received its name at birth, not, as in Moslem Egypt, at a special ceremony held a week or a fortnight later. Usually it was the mother who decided upon it, as evidenced by a New Kingdom hymn to the great state-god Amun which states: ". . . his mother who made his name".

Names of various types occur. Some, like Amenhotep, "Amun has proved to be gracious", are unconnected with the bearer, whereas others, such as Wersu, "Big is he", have attributive indications. However, in the latter case it is possible that an unmentioned god may be implied, so that we should rather translate "Great is he". Names may point to physical qualities, for instance, Pakamen, "The blind one"; or occupations: Pakapu, "The birdcatcher". Still others denote a foreign origin: Pakharu, "The Syrian" or Panehsy, "The Nubian", the latter occurring in the Old Testament as Pinehas, a son of the priest Eli, mentioned in I Samuel 1, verse 3. However, as names were inherited by children and grandchildren, they quickly lost all connection with their source. Thus not every Panehsy was a Nubian, as our surnames have similarly lost their original meaning, for how many by the name of Smith or Baker can now claim to exercise that particular profession?

Many Ancient Egyptian names are statements, wishes, or even cries uttered by the mother at the precise moment of birth. So Dhutimose (Greek: Tuthmosis), "Thoth lives", is comparable with the joyful Christian shout at Easter: "Christ has risen". Other examples of wishes and exclamations are Mersure, "May Re love him" and Aneksi, "She belongs to me". In the latter case the 'me' evidently refers to the mother. Some names, such as Yotesankh, "Her father lives", show that the baby reminded the mother of a deceased person, in this case her own husband. That other persons, for instance the 'midwives' or perhaps the father, may have been

14

present at the confinement and are responsible for giving the name, is obvious. Even a group of onlookers may do so, as the name Senetenpu, "It is our sister", proves.

An exceptional but illuminating case is contained in a New Kingdom papyrus now in Cairo. The text is the record of a lawsuit centring around the purchase of a female Syrian slave called Gem-nihiamente. This means "I found her on the West Bank" (of Thebes). It was clearly given at the moment her mistress obtained her, perhaps because the girl's original Syrian name was unpronounceable for the lady.

One specific category of names points to the actual day of birth. For instance, the appellation Mutemwia, "Mut is in the bark", that is, she makes her procession. It refers to a particular festival day when the statue of this deity was carried around by the priests, and it may be that the mother wanted in this way to keep the special occasion in memory.

It is unknown whether the Egyptians before the Late Period generally knew their day of birth. In Graeco-Roman times they certainly did, and a Twenty-first Dynasty stela already contains an indication, for it records the exact age, in years, months and days, of a man and his daughter at the moment of their decease.

From Deir el-Medina we possess several references in lists of absences to a personal feast of one of the artisans, noted down as "his feast". It was recorded since these men were then absent from their work of building the royal tomb in the Valley of the Kings. It remains uncertain, however, whether this was the celebration of a birthday. In some cases it is additionally called "his feast of Hathor", or another divinity, which seems to suggest a different reason. Once we find "his feast of his daughter", which could indeed mean her birthday. A wedding day is less plausible here, since the Egyptians never seem to have marked the beginning of a marriage relationship (see p. 109).

Normally, of course, the baby was nursed by its mother (fig. 7). This may have lasted for a long period, as a sentence from the *Instruction of Any* suggests:

When you were born after your months, (your mother) was still yoked to you, her breast was in your mouth for three years.

Painted limestone group statuette of a woman nursing her child, while a maid dresses her hair (el-Lisht, Twelfth Dynasty). (Fig. 7)

It may be that weaning was sometimes postponed since breast-feeding was even at that time believed to be an effective form of birth control. Whether a child did generally suckle for so long is uncertain.

16

Breast-feeding was, quite naturally, regarded by the mother as a pleasure. In a New Kingdom description of the joys of the scribal profession its satisfaction is compared with that of a mother who:

> has given birth and whose heart felt no distaste; she is constantly nursing her son, and her breast is in his mouth every day.

Yet, there still existed wet-nurses who took over this motherly duty, either out of necessity or to provide the puerperal woman with more rest. They occurred especially in upper class households, but not exclusively, for they are also mentioned among the inhabitants of Deir el-Medina at the end of the Ramesside Period. A scribe of this community, admittedly one of its more well-to-do members, once wrote in a letter to his son that the addressee should look well after a woman, her little daughter, and her nurse. Now in Turin is an account from the same village (also written on a papyrus), in which the recompenses a workman paid, following his wife's confinement, to a doctor and a wet-nurse are recorded. All are in tangible objects since money was not yet in existence. The payment to the woman comprised three necklaces of jasper, an ivory comb (both typical feminine items), one pair of sandals, one basket, one block of wood, and half a litre of fat. Amounting to 30½ *deben* (1 *deben* equals 90 grammes of copper), it is even higher than the value of 22 *deben* paid to the physician, who received a bronze vessel, two pairs of sandals, various baskets, one mat, and one litre of oil. Perhaps this was because she had suckled all three children of the family, which would necessitate a far longer service than that of an attendant doctor.

Wet-nurses of leading officials were highly esteemed. They were sometimes portrayed in tombs and on stelae among the daughters. Although drawn at the same scale, they are usually relegated to the very end of the row. In the early Eighteenth Dynasty tomb of the mayor Paheri at el-Kab no less than three nurses are depicted on a par with his children. Probably there was one for each daughter, since there are three girls with them. In a Middle Kingdom tomb a wet-nurse (her figure is now destroyed) is shown, together with one, or perhaps two, nannies, one of whom is holding an apotropaeic wand (see p. 10). Their names and occupations are rendered in hieroglyphic captions beside them. All this proves the close ties which existed between wet-nurses and the family. That the word for the function was the same as that for 'milchcow' may strike us as unpleasant, but this was clearly not so to the rational Egyptians.

Wet-nurses of the royal children played a particularly vital rôle (see chapter 10). For example, the career of their husbands was likely to be enhanced because of their close relationship to the royal family. A famous instance is that of Teye (see fig. 13), the wet-nurse of Nefertiti and the wife of the chariotry commander Ay, who was one of the leading figures behind the throne during the Amarna Period, and later on one of Akhenaten's successors.

Above we mentioned in passing a nanny, a related function, though less highly valued. In the *Story of the Two Brothers*, after the Queen has borne a son, it is stated that a wet-nurse and nannies were assigned to him. The word here rendered as 'nanny' is usually translated as 'attendant' or 'servant', once even 'day-nurse'. It was clearly a special female position.

The word for wet-nurse is also used for male nurses/tutors, which seems strange to modern eyes. A Middle Kingdom chamberlain, for instance, calls himself "nurse of the god (i.e. the King) in the private appartments", while a contemporary army general states that he "was indeed a support for old people, a wet-nurse of children". As the word is written with the sign of a woman suckling a baby, it is surely 'wet-nurse' that is intended. In our language, a wider meaning to the noun 'nurse' is also common.

Although a wet-nurse had her own child, and will have been chosen because of her capacity to feed two babies (unless her own had died), we nevertheless find prescriptions to stimulate her milk flow. One states that her back should be rubbed with "fish cooked in oil", which probably means: with the oil in which a fish was cooked. Other medical treatises reveal how good milk can be distinguished from bad: bad milk stinks like fish, whereas good milk smells like crushed aromatic plants. Among the advice for mother and child one text suggests grinding tips of the papyrus plant and tubers, and mixing them into the milk of a woman who has given birth to a son. The resulting concoction should be administered daily to the infant, so that it will pass day and night in a healthy slumber. Evidently this was one of the numerous popular remedies to keep a baby quiet; perhaps it did indeed work!

Mother's milk also occurs elsewhere in the pharmacopoeia as a cure for various ailments. As such it was still widely used in Coptic times. The milk of a woman who had given birth to a boy was considered to be particularly effective. A medical text designates it "the curing liquid that is in my breast", the speaker being the great mother-goddess Isis.

How was this milk stored? Over a dozen examples survive of a feminoform vessel which are all dated from the Eighteenth to Nineteenth Dynasties (fig. 8). Standing from eleven to seventeen centimetres high, they are all made of reddish-brown baked clay with the details painted black, apart from a solitary exception in steatite. Their cubic capacity at over a tenth of a litre is roughly the amount that one breast produces at one feed.

Although comparable to the anthropomorphous vases discussed in chapter 1 that contain massaging oil for the pregnant woman, the two types display completely different external characteristics. In most, but not all, of these milk containers a female holds a child, which is never represented suckling, although it sometimes reaches towards a breast which the woman may be holding and squeezing. The infant either sits on the lap or lies down upon it, or else it is carried on the back in a sling.

The woman herself is shown squatting, the habitual attitude during breast-feeding (fig. 7), as the hieroglyphic determinative employed in related words proves. She is dressed in a skirt with a fringed shawl draped over her upper torso; a suitable attire for the situation, and one which is still used in modern Egypt. Around her neck is an amulet shaped as a rising moon (figs. 8 and 9b), referring to and stimulating the milk supply. Her hair-style is conspicuously different from that of both the pregnant and the lying-in woman. The hair hangs down her back, either loosely or in a pony-tail, and two equally long tresses reach to her lap in front.

Probably this female represents a professional wet-nurse rather than the mother. On three vessels she holds an oil-horn in one hand and is dripping the contents on to her other palm. The oil would

Painted pottery vessel in the shape of a woman with a child sitting on her lap. She possibly wears a moon amulet. H. 11 cm. (Unprovenanced. Eighteenth Dynasty). (Fig. 8)

have been used to massage her back in order to stimulate the flow of milk, as in the prescription cited above. It seems likely that these objects belonged to the dispensary of a doctor, who from their shape and features could easily discern their contents, and make the distinction from the oil held in the pregnant-shaped containers.

In one instance the woman carries the baby on her back. The same position can be seen in reliefs and paintings, usually for foreigners, Nubians, Libyans, and Syrians (fig. 10a). They often transport the infant in a basket, whereas Egyptians were accustomed to place the child either on the arm or on the hip. When on the back, it was supported in a linen sling (fig. 10b). Nursing mothers hold the baby on the lap (fig. 7), or else they kneel or squat with it rest-

20

ing on their upper thigh. Representations of a woman breast-feeding while standing occur only in connection with toddlers, but are mostly confined to religious images of goddesses suckling the Pharaoh.

A baby's life in those days was threatened by many infections and maladies, infant mortality being high. Numerous instances of child burials can, of course, be cited, but we will mention only two here. Sir W.M. Flinders Petrie, the pioneer of scientific archae-ology in Egypt and Palestine, noted in his Journal of the 1889 Kahun excavations that he had found "many new-born infants . . . buried in the floors of the rooms". Clearly the inhabitants of this pyramid builders' town in the Faiyum had interred their dead babies, sometimes two or three to a box, under their house floors, usually in chests made for other purposes such as clothes or toilet equipment. At Deir el-Medina, above the village on the western slope of the Qurnet Murai, is a cemetery where more than a hun-dred children were buried, in amphorae, baskets, boxes, or proper coffins. The poorest graves were those of still-born infants, con-

(a)   *(b)*

Transporting babies: (a) Nubian woman employing a basket (Tomb of Huy (TT 40), Eighteenth Dynasty); (b) Egyptian women using slings (Tomb of Neferhotep (TT 49), Eighteenth Dynasty). (Fig. 10)

21

taining no amulets or jewellery, only one or two small vessels filled with food for the netherworld. The precarious nature of the young life is made abundantly clear in the following passage from the *Instruction of Any*:

> Do not say: 'I am too young to be taken away',
> for you do not know your death.
> When death comes he steals the infant
> from the arms of his mother,
> just like him who has reached old age.

In order to guard the vulnerable child, amuletic charms were placed around its neck. Numerous types are known and can be found in every collection of Egyptian antiquities, although it is uncertain which ones were particularly worn by new-born sucklings. A likely candidate may be the Horus-eye amulet (fig. 9a and c), safeguarding its bearer against the evil eye, a risk believed to endanger the existence of the young all over the world. The charm played a rôle comparable with that of a cross in Christian communities, especially around the Mediterranean.

Noticeable protection was also expected from small fresh papyrus rolls inscribed in cursive hieratic script. They were tightly folded and rolled into tiny packets, bound with flax and inserted into miniature cylindrical cases of wood, metal, or even gold. Worn as a pendant suspended around the child's neck on a cord, they are frequent during the centuries after the New Kingdom. As some have been discovered still bound, the texts were probably never seen by their bearers.

An early example derives from Deir el-Medina. It contains a spell against catching a common cold, the form, as is usual in these texts, being a decree by a god. In this case the Lord of the Netherworld Osiris is stated to have spoken to his vizier, the earth god Geb, in the following words:

> Erect your mast, unfold the sail, depart for the
> Iaru-fields! (the Fields of Rushes, an ideal resort in the
> hereafter). Take with you the male and the female possessor,
> the male and the female dead, who are before the face of

22

Anynakhte, son of Ubekht (the boy's mother), together with
the fever and the cold and all bad and evil things,
when they have come to him for three days.

Later texts contain guarantees to keep a boy or a girl, who is
individually named, safe from all kinds of mishaps and disasters, of
which an extensive list is presented. These may be diseases, some
like leprosy, blindness, snake and scorpion bites, being specifically
mentioned. Also cited are miseries caused by man, such as accusations and sneers. In between these common evils, misfortunes
suffered from the hands of deities and demons are listed, all mixed
up together, without an attempt at any logical order. The oracle
god undertakes to guard the child day and night, wherever it
will go, on every kind of journey, either abroad in a ship or riding along the desert edge in a chariot. He will prevent death and
give his protégé a happy infancy, he may even promise a girl that
she will conceive many children of both sexes. Protection is assured
against the magic of an Egyptian, a Nubian or a Libyan (foreigners
appear to have been especially feared), or even of a physician! Security is also provided against spirits connected with water and
watery places: canals, lakes, pools left after the recession of the
inundation, swamps, etc. These spirits seem to be similar to the
European elves.

The oracular amuletic decrees, as these papyri are called,
present us not only with a catalogue of dangers threatening the
infant's life, they also permit us insights into normal daily life.
Some are rather long, despite being compressed to a small volume,
and all are different, although containing passages that recur in
others.

From the Middle Kingdom too, cylindrical charm cases have
survived. These are either solid or hollow, and generally contain no
papyri but loose garnets and perhaps amulets. A spectacular sheet
gold over copper alloy core example, now in the Petrie Museum, is
illustrated here (fig. 11). It has been stated, ever since its discovery
in 1913 at Haraga, to be solid. However, neutron radiography,
carried out by the National Nondestructive Testing Centre, Harwell
Laboratory, was undertaken for us in 1989 and indicated a hollow
case with contents. The subsequent scientific removal of one of

23

Gold over copper core cylindrical amulet case.
Scale 2 : 1 (Tomb 211 at Haraga, Twelfth
Dynasty). (Fig. 11)

the caps has revealed three balls of copper wire and decayed organic material, perhaps papyrus. The contents are reminiscent of a particular spell on an East Berlin papyrus full of protective suggestions for mother and child, from which we have frequently quoted above. The pertinent sentences run:

> Spell for a knot for a baby: 'Are you warm in the nest?
> Are you hot in the bush? Is your mother with you?
> Is there no sister to fan you? Is there no nurse to
> afford protection?'

The first lines allude to the young god Horus who, according to the myth, passed his boyhood in the marshes of the Delta. After

24

these questions the text continues:

> Let there be brought to me pellets of gold, balls of garnet,
> a seal with a crocodile(-figure) and a hand to slay and to
> dispel the 'Sweet One' (a female demon), to warm the body,
> to slay his male or female enemy of the West (the nether-
> world). You will break out! This is a protection!

The spell is to be recited over the various items mentioned. It is
then "to be made into an amulet and put to the throat of the child.
Good!"

As throughout, such spells - some intended to promote a successful delivery, others to safeguard against children's diseases -
refer to demons. One of them, male or female, is said to enter the
house stealthily, "his nose backwards, his face averted", in order
to escape recognition. Asked whether he or she has come to kiss
the infant, to hush it, to harm it, or to take it away, the answer to
each question is the guarantee that the questioner will not permit
this to happen. Its protection is stated to be ensured additionally
with clover, garlic, honey, a fish-tail, the jawbone of a cow, and
the dorsal part of a Nile perch! Yet another spell is actually a
prayer to the sun-god Re at dawn and dusk, which has to be spoken
over the child to keep the dead away from its mother, for they
wish to snatch the babe from her breast.

All this clearly reveals just how dangerous a new-born life was
conceived to be. Fearful of all manner of evil, its mother, its wet-
nurse, and others try to conjure up the goodwill of the propitious
gods, at the same time controlling and eliminating the perils by
charms. Thus pious and magic practice go very much hand-in-hand,
as indeed they still do in present day society.

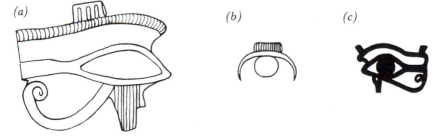

(a)   *(b)*   *(c)*

A rising moon amulet flanked by two Horus-eyes. Scale 1:1. (Fig. 9)

III   The Infant Dressed and Groomed

How were children dressed in Ancient Egypt? Our information derives mainly from reliefs, paintings and statues, but, for two reasons, these sources are not reliable. Firstly, the concept of status is all pervasive, so the actual age of the youngsters was by no means important, simply their stage in life. This implies that reality was disregarded. For example, in the Fifth Dynasty tomb of Seshemnefer III from Giza, now in Tübingen, the owner is once depicted as a naked boy with a side-lock, for there he is shown together with his deceased mother.

Secondly, these mediums are dominated by strict artistic conventions. Egyptian art was designed mainly for temples and tombs, hence it was by its very nature conservative. Thus until the New Kingdom men were mostly depicted with their upper torsos exposed. This is neither plausible for daily life, since in the winter at least it is distinctly cold in the early mornings and late evenings; nor is it confirmed by real garments that have survived. We therefore need to be suspicious when infants are represented naked.

That is in fact how they are everywhere seen during the Old Kingdom, with only a few exceptions (see fig. 26), nudity being a state which lasts right up until puberty. For instance, on a Fifth Dynasty limestone statue group, now in Hildesheim, of a woman with her son, twice represented, one of the boys standing beside his mother reaches up to her breasts. He therefore appears to be about ten years of age, and yet he is completely naked.

By contrast, in the Middle Kingdom the children are more often dressed than not, wearing the same types of clothes as their elders. Yet, this may be due to a reform in the artistic canon rather than the reflection of a change in daily habits. A clear illustration is that the boys and girls playing games (see chapter 5) are now shown clothed, whereas in the same activities on Old Kingdom tomb walls they appear nude (see figs. 23, 24, 26, 27). It may be

26

that the draughtsman indiscriminately considered them as infants and adolescents, but it seems more the effect of a difference in official style.

During the New Kingdom both nude and dressed children occur. In an Eighteenth Dynasty Theban grave a metal statuette was discovered of a naked boy, together with a far larger wooden statue of his clothed elder brother. Both pieces had been dedicated by the boys' father, and placed in their mother's coffin. It seems evident that these beloved sons had died prematurely. At what age we cannot know, but the fact that only the younger one was nude does not necessarily imply that his elder sibling was already fully adult.

In this era, as in the Old Kingdom, girls were also sometimes represented as undressed, even when they reached puberty. A painted limestone statue group of a father, mother and their daughter, now in Toulouse, shows the girl standing between her parents (fig. 12). A wide mop of hair falls down the right side of her face, and she carries a duck on her left arm (see p. 42). Although she already exhibits slight breasts, she is still naked. That girls of this age really went around exposed is doubtful. Thus the nudity may here merely indicate her status as a child.

The six daughters of the remarkable Pharaoh Akhenaten and his co-regent Queen Nefertiti are mostly shown in diaphanous dresses, exact copies of those of their mother. However, there are some exceptions among the reliefs from the royal capital at el-Amarna, in which particularly the youngest one represented is nude. In this case it can be inferred that she was indeed still a baby.

This leads us to the question of whether babies were always completely naked. It can certainly be doubted. One text, concerning Sesostris I, the second ruler of the Twelfth Dynasty, states that he already became Lord of the Two Lands before his swaddling-clothes were removed. However, the word here rendered as 'swaddling-clothes' (modern: nappies) may simply be an error of the scribe who copied the text during the Eighteenth Dynasty. His original may have run: "before the foreskin was removed", i.e., before he was circumcised (see p. 93). Yet, such a mistake is understandable if there was indeed a word for 'nappies'.

Painted limestone statue group of a seated couple and their daughter
(Unprovenanced, New Kingdom). (Fig. 12)

28

The monuments do not help us to solve the problem, for they always show babies as naked. Actual pieces of cloth in the form of linen bands have been found in large numbers, and are frequently designated by the Egyptians themselves, for example in laundry lists. However, we do not know for what purpose they were used. Although it is pure hypothesis to suggest that, in order to keep their limbs straight, Egyptian mothers wrapped their babies in swaddling-clothes, it is likely that they indeed did the same as Mary for the new-born Jesus in the stable at Bethlehem.

Returning to the Amarna princesses, there are some cases in which even the older ones among them are shown naked. A famous example is the painted plaster fragment found by Petrie on the wall of a small palace in the capital and which is now in Oxford. Part of a family scene, it shows two bald girls of different sizes sitting on cushions beside their parents, of whom only the lower limbs are preserved. The figures of three more sisters were also heavily damaged; whether they too were naked is uncertain.

Similarly, on a limestone altar slab now in West Berlin, the royal couple occurs with three of the daughters. The middle one is fondled and kissed by the father, the eldest sits on her mother's knee and looks up to her, while the youngest rests against her breast in a somewhat unnatural posture. The eldest sister wears an earring, but apart from that all three are entirely nude. In this particular case it is the difference in hair-style which provides an indication of the ages, as will be demonstrated below. That in the intimate domestic circle even older princesses went around without clothes would be an unwarranted conclusion.

This is clear from another Amarna scene, a relief on the wall of the rock-tomb of the later Pharaoh Ay (fig. 13). Akhenaten and Nefertiti here reward the faithful servant and his wife, the royal wet-nurse Teye (see p. 18) by dispensing golden goblets, collars, and other precious items, from a balcony. Three princesses accompany their parents, the elder two assisting them by also dropping necklaces at the feet of the honoured couple. Once more the girls are individually distinguished by the length of their hair. All three are nude - but so seem to be the King and the Queen, although the entire court is present, everyone being exceptionally well attired.

Ay and his wife Teye rewarded by the royal family (Tomb of Ay at el-Amarna, Eighteenth Dynasty). (Fig. 13)

The scholar who published this tomb scene in 1908 suggested that the surprising lack of modesty was due to Akhenaten's admiration of the human body. Perhaps we have to look further. Although, as we shall argue below, nudity was not considered to be shameful in Ancient Egypt, it is highly uncommon in depictions of the King. The Queen and other ladies in the Amarna Period may seem to be hardly dressed since, through their fine linen garments, the body contours are clearly visible. This is mere artistic style rather than reality. So too the undress of the royal family in this relief. It has to do with the belief, promulgated by Akhenaten, in the concept of "Living from Truth", and not with daily practice. This should warn us not to take the nakedness of the princesses at face value.

In the numerous representations from both tomb walls and stelae of the workmen's village at Deir el-Medina nudity is again encountered as the normal 'dress' of children. An obvious case is our cover illustration, from the Twentieth Dynasty tomb of Anherkhew the Younger (TT 359), one of the chief workmen of the gang of the necropolis. The owner and his wife Wabe are pictured with their four grandchildren: two older girls and a younger, and a very young boy, still a toddler. All are naked, but the lasses wear jewellery: earrings, collars, bracelets, and even armlets and anklets, the boy nothing. The only means to roughly determine their ages, apart from their height, is the difference in hair-style (see below).

In the Nineteenth Dynasty tomb from the same group, that of Sennedjem (TT 1), a banquet scene is depicted. Two girls are shown standing beside their mother, one nude, the other dressed in the flared pleated robe fashionable at that time. The first one is the smallest, but both wear their hair in exactly the same way. A couple more daughters are seen under the chairs of two female guests, obviously their mothers. They too are fully clothed in festive attire.

From these and other instances from this community we would be inclined to conclude that nudity was here permissible for girls until they reached puberty. After that, perhaps immediately after the first menstruation, it was no longer thought to be decent. It can also be suggested, on the basis of drawings on ostraca, that nakedness for boys was even more common.

Even adults, in special circumstances - such as young mothers in the confinement pavilion (see p. 4 ff.), or men engaged in particular activities, for example, fishing and fowling in the marshes - are shown without dress. This is never the case with the tomb-owners, however. It implies that in real life the Egyptians were less afraid of nakedness than we are - or perhaps one should say, used to be. Of course, the hot climate makes this understandable.

The Theban banquet scenes of the Eighteenth Dynasty, from the reign of Amenophis II onward, show nude dancers and serving wenches. It is worth noting, for the sake of comparison, that in a similar situation in the Twelfth Dynasty tomb of Antefoker and his wife Senet (TT 60) the lasses wear loincloths, although in the register below a naked lad appears. In the tomb of Rekhmire (TT 100), the vizier of Tuthmosis III, the waitresses are fully clad in long tunics. It is only immediately after this reign that nude feminine beauty becomes the norm for personnel at feasts.

For example, the lute player in the tomb of Nakht (TT 52) is dressed only in a scanty girdle, a wide collar and earrings, whereas her co-musicians, playing a harp and a double oboe, are well-covered. One case of a Theban tomb (TT 45) is particularly interesting in this respect. It was usurped after less than a century by an official from the time of Ramesses II, who ordered his painter to transform the figures of the nude girls (according to their skin colour evidently foreigners), covering them with white paint as if they were clothed. This has been interpreted as a case of prudish behaviour. However, several other alterations were made which had nothing to do with nudity but were intended to bring the scenes into accordance with the religious concepts of the tomb in that later period. Therefore to see nakedness as having been regarded as indecent is just not correct.

In view of all this it cannot surprise us that infants were more frequently rendered nude than dressed. Indeed, toddlers as well as young servants, some of them slave-boys and -girls, may have walked around without garments, at least at special occasions. That does not mean, however, that they did not possess them or wear them when it was cold. The same is true for older infants as the few surviving items of children's clothing amply demonstrate.

Of these, four are particularly interesting. The first one is a partially pleated linen dress for an older child which can claim to be the oldest surviving garment in the world and is certainly the earliest from the Nile Valley (fig. 14). It was discovered as late as 1977 in a batch of dirty rags belonging to the Petrie Museum. As the cloth derived from the large mastaba 2050 at Tarkhan in the

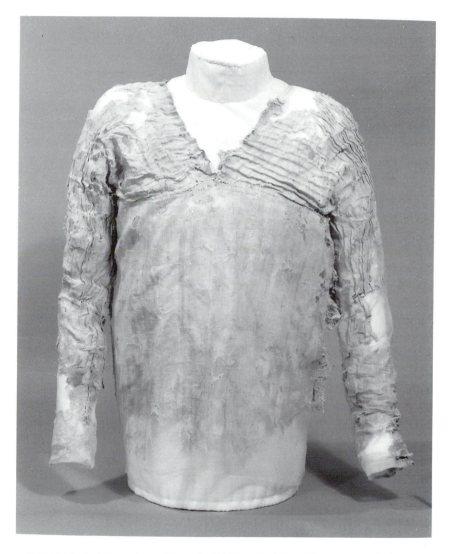

Child's pleated linen dress (Mastaba 2050 at Tarkhan, First Dynasty). (Fig. 14)

Faiyum district, the dress can be precisely dated to the reign of King Djet in the First Dynasty, about 2800 B.C. Although Petrie had not recognized it when excavating the tomb in 1912, he nevertheless fully appreciated the potential of such evidence by retaining the rags.

Splendidly conserved and mounted at the Victoria and Albert Museum, London, this garment consists of a main skirt joined selvedge to selvedge down its left-hand side with an ornamental weft fringe; no part of the hem remains. A stubbed yarn imparts an irregular grey stripe in the warp, deliberately used for decorative effect. The sleeves and yoke, cut from two pieces of material, are seamed to the top of the skirt, meeting at centre front and back to form a V-shaped neckline, edged with selvedge. Both areas display knife pleating following the line of shoulder and arm. The direction of the whipping stitches shows that the 'tailor' was right-handed. The measurements, especially of the sleeves, are those for a child of about ten years of age.

Creasing, particularly round the armpits and elbows, proves that the dress was worn in life. It had been pulled off over the head, the sleeves with their very narrow wrists following in an inverted manner, and was so discovered inside-out. Following conservation and the application of a silk crêpeline support, the entire garment was intricately turned right-side out. Each pleat having been re-ironed, the elbow crease marks were studied to determine its front and back before mounting on a frame body shaped to fit. So despite the Old Kingdom representations which would lead us to believe in the universal nakedness of infants we have here a dress which was actually part of the wardrobe of an older child.

As we have seen above, Middle Kingdom depictions often show children fully clothed and apeing their elders in fashion styles. This is confirmed by our second piece, albeit a 'false' dress consisting of the front half only. It was discovered in 1982 by a joint Hannover/Berlin expedition in the Eleventh Dynasty tomb of a young girl called Niuty at Saqqara. The cut with its skirt and separate V-shaped bodice simulates the sheath dress which was the typical garb of adult females from the Old Kingdom until the mid-Eighteenth Dynasty. Niuty's garment for the netherworld has fine tie-cords at the neck and intricate overall horizontal pleating, so no effort was spared to produce an exact model of a costume for life itself.

A pair of child's linen sleeves now in the Petrie Museum constitutes our third example (fig. 15). These pristine and beautifully made items derive from tomb 25 at New Kingdom Gurob. They are new, possibly even unworn, but were not designed as funerary equipment. Each is approximately 41 cm. in length and displays the remains of stitching at the top, indicating that they were once

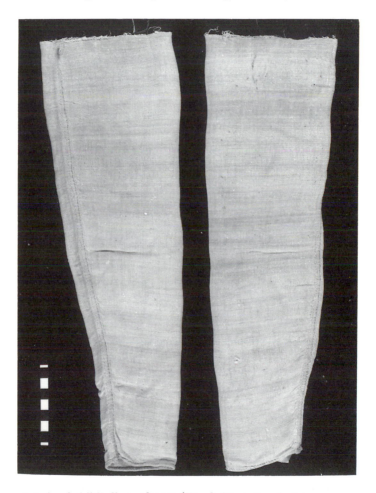

A pair of child's linen sleeves (Tomb 25 at Gurob, late Eighteenth to early Nineteenth Dynasty). (Fig. 15)

sewn into the armholes of a sleeveless tunic. This is proved by one of two children's sleeves now in Manchester, which still bears an attached shoulder fragment from a jacket. All four have run and fell seams, particularly suited to children's clothes subject to frequent wear and washing. Indeed sleeves are listed as separate items in laundry lists on Deir el-Medina ostraca. Evidently they were made separately and attached to garments only when required at times of adverse cold. Detachable sleeves are therefore by no means a new vogue of the fashion industry!

Fourthly, we have a beautiful baby's robe which belonged to Tutankhamun. Together with a shawl and a scarf, it covered the famous jackal shrine in his tomb. All three items are now in the Victoria and Albert Museum. The robe bore a hieratic docket at its bottom left-hand side which gives the date, the seventh regnal year of Akhenaten, possibly the very year of Tutankhamun's birth. This would be about 1343 B.C. We can therefore speculate that it may have been worn for a presentation ceremony at the court, and constitutes the equivalent of a modern christening robe. It does show signs of usage, the evidence of which was skilfully retained in 1986 when it underwent conservation. The linen, which is exceptionally finely spun and evenly woven, was originally bleached a pure white. It has been scientifically estimated that it would have taken three thousand hours to make or nine months of eleven-hour days! Evidently it was fit for a new-born royal prince!

In design it is a typical 'bag-tunic', one of the simplest types of garment, formed by doubling over a long length of rectangular linen with knotted fringes at each end. It is stitched up the sides, the fine over-sewing joining the two selvedges edge-to-edge, but leaving a slit for the arms. Its measurements at 1.64 metres in length by 1 metre wide mean that it is clearly a full-sized garment of adult proportions.

However, the neck-opening is only large enough to accommodate the head of a new-born baby. Conspicuously, this hole has been cut down from the fold at the shoulder, which enables it to sit well, for it would have fallen closed at the top when worn, but at the same time have parted slightly over the breastbone. The small circle has a further key-hole shaped cut ending in a point, which would have allowed it to be pulled over the head. The entire neckline is finished with a rolled hem of the most exquisite work-manship.

It is interesting here to note in passing that excavations conducted in the early 1980s at the workmen's village east of el-Amarna yielded a number of small ovals of cloth which correspond in shape to neck-openings of short-sleeved tunics. Their size suggests that they came from children's rather than adults' clothing.

Altogether Tutankhamun's wardrobe, discovered by Carter in his tomb, comprised nearly fifty child's garments and shawls, plus belts, scarfs, caps, headdresses, nearly thirty gloves, and even a fingerstall and a sling bandage. His underwear took the form of shirts, similar in design to the robe described above and also exhibiting such delicately hemmed necklines, and over a hundred triangular loincloths. These were sometimes found in sets with the basic and universally popular over-kilt. By contrast, the boy-king's cumbersome state robes show absolutely no indication of ever having been worn. This suggests that even the extant garments have to be viewed with caution, for not all present us with normal daily dress.

The most typical hair-style of Egyptian children, boys as well as girls, was a braided plait with the end rolled up in an outward-facing curl. It was worn at the right side, with the rest of the skull either shaved completely, or the hair kept very short. This haircut is found at all periods, but in the Old Kingdom it seems the most common.

An example from the late Fourth to early Fifth Dynasty is the painted limestone group statue of the crippled Seneb and his wife with their two offspring, now in Cairo, where the boy wears this plaited side-lock. The man, with his atrophied legs crossed, sits on a seat beside his wife. The sculptor has skilfully disguised the deformity by placing the chubby youngsters where, in a normal case, the legs of the man would be. Both the boy and the girl are naked, each with a finger to their mouth in accordance with the iconographic rules for infants. From this statue it appears that the side-lock was not the only possibility for children's hair, for the daughter wears hers close-cropped, like a cap over the skull. In other representations one finds girls with a pigtail hanging down their back (see fig. 18).

During the Middle Kingdom the same styles occur, but with more variants such as a wide plait falling from the crown down onto the back, or more than one pigtail. The New Kingdom fashion was for a wide mop of hair at the right side, a variation of the smaller side-lock. This is, for instance, shown in several representations of the Amarna princesses (fig. 13). Such a thick, braided mass was secured by a hair-slide, as is clearly visible in the case of the Twentieth Dynasty princes. In the tomb of Anherkhew the Younger, however, the boy and the girls all wear one, or in the case of the elder girls two, small side-locks (see cover illustration).

That such locks were indeed worn, and not a mere artistic devise, appears evident from the few well-preserved mummies of boys. A young prince, probably from the Twentieth Dynasty, and conceivably a son of Ramesses III, was found in his coffin in the Valley of Deir el-Medina. He had been abandoned there during a removal of mummies from a tomb in the Valley of the Queens to a cache, in order to escape the ever active tomb robbers. The prince still wears the wide side-lock, as does another mummy of a royal child (see p. 95), this one from the Eighteenth Dynasty. Perhaps he was a son of Amenophis II, in whose tomb his mortal remains were discovered. The first prince was, according to his body, about five years old when he died, the latter was approximately eleven.

This conspicuous hair-style was not totally restricted to children. It occurs likewise on representations of the high-priest of Ptah at Memphis, the administrative capital. It was also *en vogue* among some members of the clergy of the mortuary cults for deceased rulers at the religious capital Thebes during the New Kingdom. These are the so-called *sem*-priests who looked after the offerings for the Pharaohs, a duty that was performed for private persons by the eldest son. Hence, these priests also played that rôle, which explains why they were groomed like 'sons'.

In a Middle Kingdom tomb at Meir in Middle Egypt the daughter of the local nomarch Ukhhotep is seen with a fish-shaped piece of jewellery dangling from her side-lock (fig. 16). Several of these hair ornaments have survived from that period, executed in gold or silver with inlays of carnelian, turquoise or lapis lazuli (fig. 17b). The fish they represent is the Catfish, *Synodontis batensoda*.

38

Girl wearing a fish-shaped pendant (Tomb of Ukhhotep at Meir, Twelfth Dynasty). (Fig. 16)

The *Tales of Wonder* (see p. 4) tells a story about King Snefru. He went for a pleasure trip on a lake, his boat being manned by twenty beautiful maidens, scantily clad in see-through net-dresses. "They rowed up and down, and His Majesty's heart was happy when he saw them rowing. Then one who was at the stroke oar fingered her side-lock, and a pendant of turquoise fell into the water". The attractive crew stopped rowing, and the Pharaoh offered to replace her ornament, but the girl was adamant that she wanted her own back. A scholar was summoned, and he "placed one side of the lake's water upon the other, and found the pendant lying on a sherd".

The story admirably confirms that such jewellery was worn in the hair-lock. However, miniature fish pendants also exist that seem too small for this purpose and may have been suspended from a necklace instead. Another type of charm was even shaped like the side-lock itself (fig. 17a). They are very rare, for only eight examples are known, and how they were worn is a matter of doubt. Probably they too were attached to the bottom of the plait.

In a few instances we encounter a very peculiar hair-style consisting of three tufts on the sides and the top of the head. One of the granddaughters of Pashed, a Deir el-Medina workman of the Nineteenth Dynasty, is so groomed in one of his tomb scenes (TT 3). A grandson in the same painting wears the wide mop of hair common in that period, while both children are naked except for an earring. The unusual hair-cut of the girl is that of Nubian children (see fig. 10a). It seems to have been adopted by some Egyptian families.

Till what age was the side-lock worn? In the circumcision scene in the Sixth Dynasty tomb of Ankhmahor (see fig. 35), the boy, who from his height seems to be about twelve years old, does not wear it. Yet, other lads such as those playing the 'hut-game' in the contemporary Giza mastaba of Idu (see p. 64), are also depicted without one. It could be surmised that the lock was shaved off at the beginning of puberty, just before circumcision, as is the hair in the modern Moslem ceremony (see p. 97), but there is no proof for this theory as far as Ancient Egypt is concerned.

Above we discussed the Toulouse statue-group (fig. 12), where the girl, although already showing a feminine form, still wears the lock and is nude. A painted limestone bust of an Amarna princess, now in Paris, also displays the beginning of breasts as well as a wide side-lock, but here the child is dressed. It seems that there was no general rule for when girls were too old to go undressed *and* had to cut off their children's hair. Perhaps the latter occurred when she became nubile (see chapter 9).

In a few instances the length of the side-lock does offer an indication as to the age of the infant. On the West Berlin altar slab of the Amarna Period mentioned above, where the royal family is seen intimately together, the eldest princess wears a full, wide mop; the middle one a definitely shorter one, whereas the youngest still appears to be bald. Note, however, that the Oxford painting, also described above, shows two bald princesses, the one who

40

is definitely larger being probably not anymore a baby. For a similar instance see figure 52.

In the recompense scene in Ay's tomb (fig. 13), there is also a clear distinction between the very short lock of the youngest daughter, evidently still a toddler, the wider one of her elder sister, and the full version of the eldest. In these cases the length of the hair, based on its natural growth, is a clue for estimating their respective ages. But this is only possible when several children appear in the same representation. Moreover, as we stressed in the introduction to this chapter, it is not their actual age which is depicted, but rather the stage of life they are suggested to have reached. With the Amarna princesses that seems to be in accordance with reality, since, fortunately, we do have a rough idea of their ages, but in other cases it can be purely conventional.

Evidently, Egyptian infants wore their hair in many ways, which changed during the course of time according to the dictates of fashion. There were also various styles present at the same time. As with dress, many questions still remain unanswered, and may regrettably always be so due to the strict artistic rules which screen reality. The tangible objects: dress, human hair, and jewellery, can provide solutions, but unfortunately they have rarely survived.

(a)   *(b)*

Children's jewellery: (a) electrum side-lock pendant. Both sides, scale 1 : 1 (Unprovenanced, Middle Kingdom); (b) gold catfish hair ornament. Scale 1 : 1 (Tomb 72 at Haraga, Twelfth Dynasty). (Fig. 17)

IV   The Realm of Childhood

An insight into the upbringing of children in Ancient Egypt can be afforded by a study of the tomb scenes, surviving artefacts, and textual evidence. These sources reveal that youngsters kept pets, owned toys, participated in games (chapter 5), and were gradually introduced into the adult world by rôle play. Although earlier at work alongside their parents, they could still, on occasions, be as badly behaved as their modern counterparts.

The Ancient Egyptians are renowned for their love of animals. Dogs were man's faithful companions, cats are often depicted under the chair of their mistresses, while monkeys with their clownish antics and capacity for imitation amused their owners.

Therefore, it does not surprise us that children are frequently represented with their pets. Some New Kingdom wooden and ivory mirror handles are carved in the form of young girls who hold animals on their arms. Kittens are depicted on examples in Bolton and East Berlin, and on a handle, now in Bologna, a small duck nestles in the child's left hand which rests in front of her breast. A bird is similarly nursed by the girl on the Toulouse statue (see fig. 12).

Indeed, birds are fairly commonly represented as children's pets. In the Fifth Dynasty tomb of Nefer and Kahay at Saqqara, for instance, a naked girl with a pigtail (see for this hair-style p. 38) holds a lapwing by its wing (fig. 18). In the Middle Kingdom tomb of Ukhhotep at Meir, the owner's daughter, mentioned above in connection with the fish-ornament dangling from her side-lock (see p. 38), stretches out her left hand. In this she grasps a lotus-flower on which a pigeon is perched (see fig. 16).

Boys are often shown clutching a hoopoe in one hand, a bird that becomes tame in captivity and attracts the attention of youngsters by its gaily coloured plumage. Pigeons were also kept by boys, as attested by reliefs in the famous Fifth Dynasty mastaba of Ti at

Nefer, with his pet dog, accompanied by his nude daughter who clutches a lapwing (Mastaba of Nefer at Saqqara, Fifth Dynasty). (Fig. 18)

43

Saqqara. They are held by the two elder girls in the family scene in the Twentieth Dynasty tomb of Anherkhew the Younger (TT 359) (see cover illustration). The Nineteenth Dynasty tomb of Senne-djem (TT 1), also from Deir el-Medina, depicts a girl in a flared robe who has what appears to be the Egyptian or Nile goose in her grip. The same bird occurs in children's hands on some stelae from this site. Whether in such New Kingdom instances these animals, which could be aggresive towards men, were indeed pets, or rather offerings, is not quite clear. This is especially so in view of another painting in Sennedjem's tomb where adults are carrying geese, which in this case are probably intended for sacrificial purposes.

An unusual scene is found in the tomb of the courtier Mery-re II at el-Amarna. Six royal princesses are here depicted standing in two rows in a kiosk behind their parents' throne. Of the younger ones, in the bottom row, both the first and the second each carry a young gazelle, while the last girl tickles the animal held by her sister. The representation is conspicuous since gazelles in general cannot be domesticated, although other equally untameable animals, such as antelopes and ibexes, are known to have been kept in the North Palace at el-Amarna. These wild beasts do not usually return signs of affection, as kittens, for example, are accustomed to do.

Egyptian children played with toys, as do infants all over the world. Not with the sophisticated kinds as are presented to them in modern society, although, as we shall see, some were of principally the same type as in our age. Excavations have brought to light objects which were certainly, and in some instances probably, made to amuse the youngsters.

Particularly in the Middle Kingdom town of Kahun several toys have been found. For instance, there are balls, made either of wood or segments of leather sewn together, and stuffed with dried grass or barley husks. One of the latter type, now in Manchester, had obviously cracked and subsequently been carefully re-stitched, demonstrating that it was a valued possession. Painted reed and linen balls are known from other sites (fig. 19). For the various games that especially girls played with them, see chapter 5.

Kahun has also yielded whip tops, ranging from 2½ to over 7 centimetres in height. They are circular pieces of wood flattened

44

at one end and pointed at the other. Examples in blue faience (a glazed composition) have been found elsewhere (fig. 19). A special type of toy from Kahun consists of long wooden sticks, measuring up to 16 centimetres, which are pointed at both ends. These were tip cats, which were thrown into the air and hit with a stick or a club before they fell on the ground. The child who managed to hit the 'cat' the furthest was the winner. This game is still played in the United Kingdom in Lancashire where it is called 'Piggy', while a different version, with complicated rules, occurs in modern Egypt.

Already from Prehistory we find proof for another pastime. In a child's grave, number 100 at Naqada, Petrie found a complete set of nine calcite and breccia skittles, with four porphyry balls and a small gate made up of three marble bars through which the balls had to be rolled. This group is now in Oxford. Parts of a similar game, from another tomb at Naqada, are in the Petrie Museum. It consists of sixteen balls (ten being of limestone, four of porph-

Children's toys: (above) left and right, painted reed and linen balls (Unprovenanced, Roman Period); (centre) blue faience tops (Faiyum, Roman Period); (below) wooden feline with crystal eyes and a moveable jaw fitted with bronze teeth (Thebes, New Kingdom). (Fig. 19)

45

yry, and two of breccia) and one porphyry bar from a similar gate, but no skittles.

From many sites small animal figures, roughly modelled from Nile mud, are known. They comprise hippopotami, crocodiles, cattle, sheep, pigs, monkeys and apes, etc. A particularly fine example is the pack donkey now in New York. It was discovered by the Earl of Carnarvon's expedition in the area of Deir el-Bahri, and dates from the Second Intermediate Period. The nine clay sacks which the animal carries are supported by four vine-leaf stalks thrust into the body of the beast. Although this is indeed most probably a children's toy, not all clay figures were made for or by youngsters. Some were plainly votive offerings.

The exact nature of numerous doll figures is equally uncertain. Very probably most rag dolls were the possessions of girls, perhaps also of boys. Some even have their own accompanying wardrobes, comprising several changes of outfit. A clear indication that the human figure was indeed a toy is when it was found in a child's grave. An example is the wooden doll with moveable arms from the Twelfth Dynasty tomb of the girl Sitrennut at Hawara (fig. 20). A carefully made wooden model bed was also discovered in this burial, perhaps for the same doll. The entire tomb group is now in the Petrie Museum.

Other specific female figures, however, are the so-called 'concubines' (see p. 7), magical representations intended to stimulate fertility, and therefore placed in a funerary context. In these the genitalia are mostly emphasized, which clearly distinguishes them from girls' dolls.

In Kahun too some painted wooden puppets with moveable limbs were found, like that belonging to Sitrennut. Moreover, Petrie discovered in one house a large stock of doll's hair, consisting of fine flax threads, about 15 centimetres in length, placed together and rolled with mud, which would have been inserted into holes in the figure's head. (Sitrennut's doll was found with such a wig, which was unfortunately lost soon after discovery). Hence this building at Kahun has been dubbed 'the toy-maker's shop'.

More intricate still than dolls with loose limbs are some jumping jacks. In West Berlin there is a wooden crocodile with a moveable lower jaw, and in the British Museum are similar figures of

46

Painted wooden doll with moveable arms. She originally had a wig of mud beads (Tomb 58 at Hawara, Twelfth Dynasty). (Fig. 20)

both a mouse and a feline (fig. 19). Leiden has a crude wooden human figure with outstretched arms which, when a cord is pulled, moves up and down on a board as if grinding corn.

Somewhat doubtful is the purpose of a New Kingdom wooden model boat on wheels, discovered by Petrie in a tomb at the town of Gurob in the Faiyum, and now in the Petrie Museum. A very fragile object, it was found in pieces and subsequently reconstructed. On the bow is what seems to be a ramming device, in the centre on relatively long poles a light awning, and at starboard a steering oar. It has been suggested that it was originally a funerary boat, intended for a grave, and was later adapted for use as a toy by adding the wheels. Ships on wheels are very rarely depicted, just as generally vehicles on four wheels seldom occur. Tuthmosis III mentions in the report on his Syrian campaigns at Karnak that his transport-ships were placed on waggons pulled by oxen, and a few representations of two- and four-wheeled carts do exist, proving that they were not quite unknown. So it may indeed be that someone put a funerary boat on an under-carriage for the amusement of a child. The delicate object was perhaps rather more ornamental than an actual plaything.

One exceptional and splendid toy deserves a more extensive description. It was excavated in the Middle Kingdom tomb of a girl called Hapy at el-Lisht, in the Faiyum district, and consists of four small ivory figures, about 6 centimetres high. One is a loose piece, now in New York, and three, now in Cairo, are together placed on a rectangular base. All four stand on round, 'spoon'-shaped, pierced bases. They represent naked dancing pygmies. The loose one puts his hands together in a gesture of clapping, the three others hold them with their palms outwards at shoulder level. All four have bowed legs. Their bases were placed in boxes which are also pierced. When strings were attached to the figures and threaded through the holes, they caused, when pulled, jerking movements of the dancers, even to the sophistication of full pirouettes.

Pygmies were famed in Ancient Egypt for their special dances. In the *Pyramid Texts* (spells for the deceased king) a sentence occurs stating: "He is a pigmy of the divine dances, who diverts the god in front of the Great Throne". During the Sixth Dynasty

48

an expedition leader named Harkhuf brought back from Nubia such a pygmy, as had been done earlier by another traveller for King Isesi of the Fifth Dynasty. When Harkhuf sent a message about his journey to the Pharaoh, Pepi II, who was still a boy, the youthful ruler was so enthusiastic at the prospect of possessing the dwarf that he wrote by his own hand a letter to his emissary. He urged him to bring the African quickly and safely to the court at Memphis, for "My Majesty desires to see this pygmy more than the gifts of Sinai and Punt". This private letter was evidently considered a high honour by its recipient, who had a copy inscribed on the outer wall of his tomb at Qubbet el-Hawa, opposite Aswan. So we still know the story.

Against this background it is clear why the ivory dancing pygmies with their expressive faces constituted not only a sophisticated, but also a highly prized toy. So treasured in fact, that already in antiquity it was painstakingly repaired with tiny dowels. Whether, however, its child owner even played with it looks doubtful. Its material, ingenious construction, and fairly fragile structure, all rather suggest an object for grown-ups.

A child's life, in those times, was not completely filled by playing. It also contained a gradual introduction into work as an adult, a process which began at an earlier stage than in our society. This is understandable, for the majority of the youngsters, and virtually all girls, never attended a school. So they had all the opportunity, first as a natural matter for fun by rôle play, and progressively more seriously, of taking part in their parents' activities, at home, in the fields, and in the workshops.

That is still the case in the rural areas of modern Egypt, although formal education now extends to a large part of the youth. Already from the age of three onward, boys run errands and feed animals. As the Egyptians say, this period in life is for them "to be moistened with earth". From about seven years of age on their help becomes more important, and at twelve they fulfil essential duties in the tilling of the fields. Girls are also sent out at an early age on errands, and get to perform small chores in the house, in the preparation of food, for instance, or attending to poultry or sheep. Later on, after reaching approximately their seventh birthday, they help in baking bread and collecting fuel for the oven. At all ages children, particularly girls, but boys as well, are supposed to look after their younger siblings. Doubtless the same would have held true in Pharaonic times.

In the representations on the tomb walls we encounter, for instance, juveniles when they bring offerings to the gods and the deceased in the company of their parents. On some New Kingdom stelae from Abydos a boy or a girl is depicted adoring Osiris, together with adults. Similarly they appear in the tomb chapels of Deir el-Medina in adoration scenes.

According to their nature children are accustomed to imitate their elders. So we see girls among the female mourners at funerals, in the same attitudes as their mothers and elder sisters, doubtlessly uttering the same shrill wailing cries. A famous instance occurs in the Theban tomb of the vizier Ramose (TT 55), of the Eighteenth Dynasty, where in the painted scene of the funeral cortège a naked girl is depicted with her hands in the same typical gesture as the elder women. A similar representation occurs in the roughly contemporaneous Theban tomb of Neferhotep (TT 49) (see fig. 10b).

Boys too imitated their elders, as can be seen on a New Kingdom stela now in Turin. Two sisters are kneeling before an offering stand, at the other side of which the deceased housewife, very probably their mother, is seated. Behind them squats their younger brother, who holds his arms in an attitude of mourning similar to that of one of his sisters. The youngest sibling, still an infant for she is rendered naked, brings up the rear and apes her seniors.

At an early age children started to help their parents. A New Kingdom proverbial expression states: "You shall not spare your body when you are young; food comes about by the hands, provision by the feet". The representations show girls looking after their younger brothers and sisters, and, like their mothers, carrying them in a sling (see fig. 10b). A sentence from a spell quoted above (see p. 24): "Is there no sister to fan you?", is also of relevance here.

Boys, but also girls, are depicted in agricultural scenes engaged, for instance, in gleaning. This is shown in the Eighteenth Dynasty Theban tomb of Djeserkareseneb (TT 38), where a boy and a girl are seen, beside each other (but drawn, according to the Egyptian artistic conventions, above each other), picking up the ears amidst high standing corn. They put the gleanings in a basket which they carry on their arm.

In Old Kingdom tomb scenes we find particularly boys watching flocks or tending cattle, thereby assisting the herdsmen. In the Fifth Dynasty mastaba of Hetepherakhet, now in Leiden, a naked boy hands up a vessel to an adult for the latter to drink from. A similar gesture occurs in another relief from the same tomb, but in this case the action takes place on a cargo-boat on the river. In the Middle Kingdom tomb of Pepiankh at Meir a kitchen hut is represented (fig. 21). On the right a man is busy roasting a duck on a spit over a brazier, fanning the glowing charcoal with his other hand. Above him, joints of meat and a duck are hanging on a line. His companion to the left, who is also squatting, tucks into a piece of meat. Between them a boy is standing who carries a pot in his right hand and in his left an unidentified object. The fellow on the left orders him: "Get to work, that you may summon the lads to

In a kitchen hut one man is at work while his companion, who is eating, orders a boy to run an errand. The hieroglyphs give the lad's answer: "I'll do it" (Tomb of Pepiankh at Meir, Twelfth Dynasty). (Fig. 21)

eat", whereupon he answers: "I'll do it".

Evidently the boy had his own duties in the kitchen, apart from running errands. From a New Kingdom 'schoolbook' we learn that the baker, in the act of placing bread on the fire, puts his head into the oven, while his son holds his feet. "In the event of slipping from his son's hand, he thereby falls down into the oven's bottom". Such a child bore a heavy responsibility!

In the Nineteenth Dynasty tomb of Ipuy (TT 217) at Deir el-Medina we find a boy chasing birds from a heap of grain, also a type of simple 'work'. Other scenes of that period depict youngsters assisting at ploughing, or themselves sowing, and a text describes the personnel of a vineyard as consisting of seven men, four adolescents, four old men, and six children, totalling twenty-one.

All this demonstrates that the economic importance of even fairly young children was not negligible for the households of the poor. In the case of the upper classes, however, it would have been the slaves or servants who performed the minor duties. In the Eighteenth Dynasty Theban tomb of a certain User (TT 260) there is a scene of a nude girl arranging cushions on a chair, under the supervision of an elder servant. In the register above another lass smoothes down the linen on a bed. A similar representation, but badly damaged, occurs in the contemporary Theban tomb of Amenemhat (TT 82); enough has been preserved to allow us to surmise that she is also making the bed.

As in these cases, the girls assisting their mistress at the toilet may also have been slaves, and the same holds true for those nude beauties serving at banquets in many Eighteenth Dynasty tombs. In one instance such a 'waitress' even washes her hands before handing out food and drink. Whether the dancing girls or those in the orchestra at the festival meals (see p. 32) were free citizens or not is uncertain.

Boys are rarely represented as dancers, but one at least occurs, accompanied by an all female orchestra, in the tomb of Neferhotep (TT 49), while another infant, perhaps still very young, waves a branch. On the same wall are seen two nude Nubian boys, recognizable from their striking hair-style, and wearing earrings. They walk among the ladies accompanying Neferhotep's wife when she leaves the palace after an audience. Although these tiny

52

A boy and a girl threatened by an irate doorkeeper while their nanny drinks from a jar. Part of a scene in which a lady is received by the Pharaoh Ay in the palace gardens (Tomb of Neferhotep (TT 49), Eighteenth Dynasty). (Fig. 22)

boys were probably indeed slaves, they seem to have been kept almost as pets.

In the Deir el-Medina tomb of the sculptor Ken (TT 4), dating from the Nineteenth Dynasty, a girl, carrying a baby in a sling, is depicted in a funeral procession, conspicuously wearing the 'Nubian' hair with tufts. As such a cut did indeed occur in some Egyptian families among the necropolis workmen (see p. 40), it remains uncertain whether she was a young member of the family or a slave.

Since such servants, whether free or not, appear to have been fairly young, their performance can hardly have been impressive. That this was felt to be so according to the Egyptians themselves is amply demonstrated by an early Eighteenth Dynasty letter. The author asks a high official why his female servant, who was with him, has been taken away, for "she is a child and cannot work".

All these instances of more or less serious activities do not mean that children did not play, as appears from their toys; nor that they were always well-behaved and helpful. In the famous Eighteenth Dynasty Theban tomb of Menna (TT 69) we see two girls in a corn-field who are quarrelling and trying to tear out each other's hair. In the register below this others are depicted in a more friendly pursuit. One sits, leaning back and stretching out her bare foot, while her companion examines it, probably attempting to pull out a thorn.

The much cited tomb of Neferhotep (TT 49) gives us a delightful picture of naughtiness (fig. 22). While the wife of the official is received by King Ay in his garden house, she is followed by a train of well-dressed female servants. The last figure in the row, very probably a nanny, lags somewhat behind. Obviously the day had been hot and the children had worn her out, so she is happy to be able to gulp down a draught of beer from a jar. Meanwhile her charges, a boy and a girl, both of whom are naked, have teased a doorkeeper, who appears from a gate brandishing a stick.

If all the representations of infants seriously occupied seem to render a stern picture of their life, these last scenes show that the realm of childhood was, as might be expected, the same in Ancient Egypt as in all other times and cultures.

V   Games

In a small number of Old and Middle Kingdom tombs several representations occur of different games, played by boys and girls. With a few notable exceptions (see below) the two sexes are never portrayed together. In this connection it is interesting to note that neither are there any mixed groups of players in Upper Egypt at the present time. In the Old Kingdom scenes it is clearly lads and lasses who are shown, the boys being sometimes, although not always, distinguished by their side-locks, and in all cases naked. In the Middle Kingdom the age is less evident; perhaps children as well as adolescents are here depicted (see pp. 26-27).

Some of the games we would term 'acrobatics' or even 'dancing'; most, at least, were 'athletics'. Yet, there is nothing like the physical education of the Greeks or of modern times. Genuine sports are only for specific groups, especially for soldiers as a requisite part of their drill, and in this category New Kingdom princes and their companions should also be included (see chapter 10). Exercises are also characteristic in the training of professional dancers.

It is not always clear why the games were featured on tomb walls, and what the deeper meaning was that motivated their portrayal. They are certainly not simply pictures of daily life, but rather connected with religion and the afterlife. In addition, the games have been generally supposed to possess didactic contents as a preparation for adult life, and a psychological aspect concerned with the repression of sexuality.

Acrobatics, closely connected with dancing, played a rôle in the cult. An example are the scenes of girls turning back flips or somersaults. A group of four such lasses, resting on both their hands and feet with either their backs or fronts bowed upwards in an arch, occurs on the Red Chapel of Hatshepsut in the Karnak Temple. On the same walls is another group of six, and in the

Luxor Temple even twelve are shown. Each time they are accompanied by musicians, playing harps and sistra (Egyptian rattles), and they clearly form part of a procession.

It may be that the girls are not children any more, but young professional dancers. Such acrobatics, however, had to be gradually learnt. In the Middle Kingdom tombs of the nomarchs Baqt and Kheti at Beni Hasan these exercises are represented, in which girls help each other to turn head over heels in a somersault. One picture shows two stages, another three.

Although only girls seem to have 'danced' at religious occasions, boys also mastered the skill, though they never turn somersaults. The tomb of Amenemhat at Beni Hasan shows them engaged, during the transport of a statue, in a pirouette, several stages being depicted beside each other in the form of a strip cartoon. In another scene in the same register a boy turns cartwheels, ending up standing upon the back of a crouching friend.

Other types of physical exercises include balancing acts. For instance, a boy is standing on his head, his arms crossed over his chest. Elsewhere three lads carry a fourth on their shoulders (fig. 23b). The 'donkey-game' appears in an Old Kingdom scene where

(a)   (b)

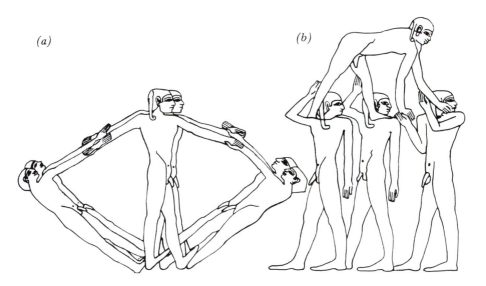

Boys' games: (a) star game; (b) balancing act (Mastaba of Ptahhotep at Saqqara, Fifth Dynasty). (Fig. 23)

56

an older boy on all fours carries two small children on his back. They are poised one at each side, precariously hanging like sacks on a donkey, so that they have to clutch each other firmly in order to keep balance. This would require considerable strength for a toddler.

A conspicuous counterpoising activity, represented in Old and Middle Kingdom tombs, has been dubbed by scholars the 'star-game' (fig. 23a). Its Ancient Egyptian name is 'erecting the wine-arbour'. Two boys are standing in the middle, holding with outstretched arms two, or even four others, who lean back balancing on their heels. They are spun around as quickly as possible. This is one case in which, in a single representation, boys and girls play together, for four lasses are rotated by two standing lads.

Equally obvious is the game known under its modern Arabic name *khazza lawizza* or 'jumping over the goose' (fig. 24a). It is still played in Egypt and in the Near East. Two boys are sitting, face to face, each putting his feet and his hands with outstretched fingers in a tier upon each other. So they form a living hurdle over which a third lad has to leap. In modern times the seated boys keep their feet wide apart; the trick here is therefore not only to jump high but also far enough. That may likewise be the case in the Sixth Dynasty mastaba (free-standing tomb) of Ptahhotep at Saqqara, where the seated boys are shown side by side, and a third during his run (fig. 24a). He has to spring over the hands and the feet of both friends in a single bound, or, after alighting midway between the two, he must leap again.

The Middle Kingdom representations of wrestling are famous. They occur in three different tombs at Beni Hasan, namely those of Amenemhat, Baqt III, and Kheti, where each time a large part of a wall is covered with figures in various stances. In order to easily distinguish the contestants one is coloured a darker reddish-brown than the other. They grasp each other around the waist, lift each other bodily from the ground, and even hold one another upside-down, until one lies prone on the floor.

That wrestling was popular appears evident from various small three-dimensional groups of the Middle Kingdom. The sport is also pictured on a New Kingdom Deir el-Medina ostracon, now in Cairo. In this case, however, it is soldiers who are exercising, not

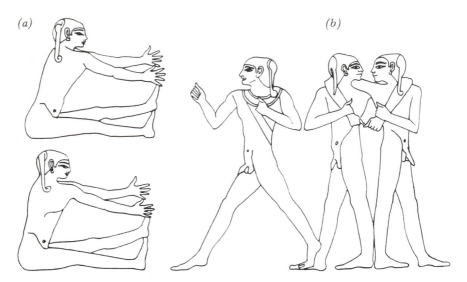

(a)   *(b)*

Boys' games: (a) 'khazza lawizza'; (b) ? stampers (Mastaba of Ptahhotep at Saqqara, Fifth Dynasty). (Fig. 24)

children. On the other hand, the scenes in the Old Kingdom tomb of Ptahhotep clearly represent young boys, as their side-locks prove.

The unique Fifth-Sixth Dynasty limestone group now in Chicago and illustrated here (fig. 25) has been called a wrestling scene, but this is not quite certain. In a most unusual mixture of the sexes a naked boy stands astride the neck and shoulders of a clothed girl. His knees are slightly bent and he leans a little forward. His hands, which lie on her back, grasp an unknown object, and he gazes straight ahead. The girl is kneeling beneath him resting on her hands, knees and toes. Very exceptionally in Egyptian art, her head is turned aside and upward, looking at the boy's back. A similar attitude is seen in the Fifth Dynasty mastaba of Hetepherakhet, now in Leiden, but there a man is beating a boy, perhaps in fun, which is clearly not the case in the Chicago group. It could be a version of leap-frog, that all time favourite pastime, which is here depicted.

Another contest, and one that is also still universally played, was that of tug-of-war. It is represented in the Sixth Dynasty mastaba of Mereruka at Saqqara, albeit without a rope, and is one

58

Painted limestone group statuette of a boy and a girl playing (Tomb of Ny-kau-inpu at Giza, Fifth to Sixth Dynasty). (Fig. 25)

59

of the very rare team games. Two lines of three boys stand facing each other. The captains grasp each other by the wrists, each placing one foot resting on its heel against that of his opponent, while their upper bodies lean backwards. Behind them the other two are standing, each holding the one in front with both hands around his waist, so forming a human chain. At a given command they begin to pull. The shouts of the team members are rendered in hieroglyphic captions above each group as: "Your arm is much stronger than he. Don't give in to him", to which the opposing party retorts: "My side is stronger than yours. Hold them firmly, my friend".

A game that is still popular in Britain is that of 'elbows'. The two contestants, sitting face to face, put their right elbows on a table and clasp each other's right hand so that their forearms are vertically aligned against each other. The aim is to force the partner's forearm back onto the table by brute strength. In Ancient Egypt what looks to be a variant was played standing up. The boys interlock their hands behind their necks, averting their faces. They try to hit each other's elbow so as to knock the opponent off-balance.

In certain Middle Kingdom tombs girls' games with balls (see fig. 19) are represented. So we see them juggling with three balls, trying to keep them in the air by quickly throwing each one up, while the other two are still in momentum. A more difficult version is played with the arms crossed. On a satirical ostracon from Deir el-Medina, now in Stockholm, a mouse performs the same feat, but with only two balls (fig. 26). Perhaps she took them from the chest in front of her. At any rate, she looks well-pleased with her achievement!

Another trick involves passing balls to each other while riding piggy-back on a partner. Yet another is rhythmic throwing, performed in a group with four girls who stand around clapping their hands, while two others toss and catch three balls in rotation.

It may be that these amusements were partly exercises for cult games. We can even doubt whether the players were indeed young children, for they exhibit a special hair-style, that of pigtails with a tassel at the ends, which seems to belong to the official costume of dancers.

60

*Painted limestone ostracon showing a mouse juggling with
two balls (Deir el-Medina, New Kingdom). (Pl. 26)*

A ritual ball game is indeed known from the monuments,
where it is played by the Pharaoh in the presence of a female deity.
He hits the ball with a stick or club, not unlike the batsman at
cricket, while two priests attempt to make a catch. The goddesses,
such as Hathor, are all connected with the concept of 'love', and
the caption speaks of enjoyment. Moreover, this scene, as far as
the Luxor Temple is concerned, is located in the Birth Chamber. It
seems that a rite alluding to the sacred marriage of the Pharaoh
and a goddess is here depicted.

This is far removed from our dexterous girls. Yet, they too
may be involved in, or exercising for, a ritual performance. Already
in the Old Kingdom *Pyramid Texts* mention is made of a ball game
for the entertainment of the deceased.

Apart from athletic activities, there are also some of a much
more sedentary nature. Surprisingly, they are never board-games,

61

although these were widely indulged in by adults. Instead we have guessing games. For instance, a boy kneels on all fours with his eyes closed, while one of his two companions pokes him in the back. He has each time to guess which one has hit him. A similar version has been popular in Britain for centuries and is known under many names, such as 'Stroking the baby' or 'Hot cockles'. It is the same diversion that the guards used to taunt the blindfolded Jesus with when in the house of the high priest on the night before the Crucifixion.

Another gambling contest may have been played with four pots upside-down, the two competitors sitting at opposite sides. One of them secretes an object, perhaps a stone, under one of the vessels, and the other has to guess under which it is hidden. However, it must be admitted that this interpretation of the scene is somewhat hypothetical. As the explanatory caption is a completely unknown word, there is some doubt as to whether this was indeed the purpose.

Easily recognizable are games such as 'territories' and 'flashing figures'. In the former two boys throw pointed sticks in sequence. They land upright in what appears to be a square sandpit. In the modern version the aim is to draw a line through the place where the dart fell in order to cut off a segment from the other's territory. Whether something similar is intended here is unclear. In the latter game one player calls out, according to the caption, "say it", i.e., 'guess', whereupon he opens his hand. The number of extended fingers decides who wins. If the guess is correct the two change places. Several variations occur in present day Britain, for instance that of 'Finger and Thumb'. It is also similar to the Italian 'Mora', which is especially used in deciding who will be 'he' or 'it', i.e., the odd man out.

Most of the activities discussed so far involve two participants, others being solely spectators. They are of the duelling, the exerting, or the guessing types. Games of chasing, such as 'Touch' or 'Tig'; of catching, like 'Farmer, Farmer, may we cross your golden river?'; or seeking, notably 'Hide-and-seek', with all their possible variations, are simply not recognized on the tomb walls. Nevertheless, this does not mean that they were not played in real life.

62

At least one pretending game, a variety of 'Cops and Robbers', does occur. In the Old Kingdom mastabas of Ptahhotep, Mereruka, and Khentika/Ikhekhi at Saqqara, a bound captive, his elbows tied behind his back, is led away on a cord by a group of other naked boys. The caption runs: "Come, vagabond, who has followed his desire. If another one sees this, he is afraid".

Also of a make-believe character is the 'hut-game', a name coined by Egyptologists. It is clearly shown on a limestone block from an Old Kingdom tomb, probably at Giza, which is now in the British Museum (fig. 27). On the right of the central register are five boys, all with side-locks and naked, apart from the middle figure who is clad in a loin-cloth. Four of them are enclosed by a double line with rounded corners, which may represent a structure such as a hut, but may also depict, in plan, a cord or a narrow ditch. The two youngsters at the right are standing, with one hand raised. A third one, the principal figure, is stretched out on the ground and puts one hand through or over the enclosure, while a fourth is bending over him and seems to pin him down. The fifth stands outside the enclosure, and appears to be touching it with

Painted limestone relief: (centre register) left, a fertility dance; right, the 'hut game' (? Giza, late Fifth to early Sixth Dynasty). (Fig. 27)

63

one hand. The caption over the scene runs: "Rescue you alone from it, my friend", meaning "you should attempt to escape from the enclosure alone".

A second instance of this game occurs in the Sixth Dynasty Giza mastaba of Idu. It is almost identical, except for small variations such as the absence of the side-locks and the loin-cloth of the bending figure. Above the head of the boy outside the enclosure are the additional words: "I shall rescue you". So despite what the others within say, this lad offers help to his companion.

The third example is a more vigorous interpretation found in the Middle Kingdom tomb of Baqt III at Beni Hasan. Here, however, there are several deviations from the earlier two: no enclosure, no side-locks, and all the participants are clothed in short kilts. The one 'outside' is held back by two others who grasp his arm, while the prostrate youth seems to be pinned down by force. The figures at the right-hand side are missing. That it is nonetheless a rendering of the same scene is apparent from the caption, which is practically identical.

The absence of an enclosure raises the question of how essential this detail was to the 'game', the exact rules of which are unknown. It was, however, particularly on account of this feature, which was interpreted as a 'hut', that a suggestion has been made that the activity was derived from puberty rituals, for huts and enclosures are a facet of such ceremonies among several African peoples. However, the argument is very weak, and the lack of this particular detail in the later tomb could simply be an indication of variations that children's games are apt to show at different times and places.

In the mastaba of Idu the activity seems connected with what two girls right of the 'hut' are doing, for the pigtail of one of them is hanging over the double line of the enclosure. Note that this can also be seen in the British Museum relief, although the child herself is lost (fig. 27). The lasses in Idu's tomb are standing, each with one arm on the other's shoulder. The caption above runs: "Linking the linkers", but what this means is obscure. An almost identical representation occurs in Ptahhotep's tomb of two boys (fig. 24b). Unfortunately the inscription here is equally cryptic, but a kind of 'scuffle' appears to be pictured, in which one lad attempts to knock the other down. Perhaps it is a version of the modern 'Stampers', where two contestants place their hands on each other's shoulders and stamp as hard and as many times as possible on the other's feet.

A final instance of a boys' games may actually be a ritual, although it is executed by youngsters and is juxtaposed to the 'hut' scene. It is a unique instance, showing dancing around a fertility figure, and occurs on the left-hand side of the central register of our, by now familiar, British Museum block (fig. 27).

Five naked boys, with side-locks, hold a staff in their right and what may be a reed-stalk or ear of grain in their left hands. They are running or cavorting around a central motionless figure. This also seems to be a lad, although the three strips of cloth hanging from his girdle veil his sex. In his right palm he holds a stick terminating in a hand, a sign of (low) authority. Most conspicuous is his head, which is covered by a mask. That it is indeed a disguise appears evident from the youth's lack of a neck, for it rests directly on his shoulders. The large tripartite wig is surmounted by two pointed, triangular ears. The human face, seen of course in profile, features a prominent nose, an enormous eye, and two horizontal grooves above the eyebrows. It is significant that, whereas all the figures in this scene, as well as in the 'hut-game', still show clear traces of reddish-brown pigment, the masked one is uncoloured. Possibly it was originally painted white.

Although suggestions have been made that the disguise represents the lion-eared god Bes (see fig. 2a), a more convincing argument is to see in the erect ears a genet rather than a lion or a leopard. The costume is one that connects the figure with lower rank fertility divinities, possibly a specific vintage deity. Therefore, the masked boy alludes to fertility, and the dance around him may depict a fecundity or harvest ritual, in connection, perhaps, with the reaping scene in the lower register. This would be more likely if the youngsters did indeed carry ears of corn. The accompanying caption, which probably reads: "Dancing by a group of children", sheds no light on the interpretation of the scene.

Some of these games clearly had the function of preparing the participants for adult life, either physically or, albeit seldom, mentally. So 'Cops and Robbers', as described above, evidently has the task of teaching the children that the law and order of the community should be maintained. This aspect may explain why the scene was depicted on the walls of three Old Kingdom tombs; clearly it had here a deeper significance than simply that of youngsters having fun. Such is also clear from the fertility dance, but in other cases, like the 'hut-game', the reason for its representation is just not explicit. Yet, there must have been a more profound meaning than that which meets the eye on the level of everyday activities. At least this will have been so in the conception of the artists and the tomb-owners who chose to have them represented. But what that implication may be is pure hypothesis. In the meantime, such scenes present us with tantalising glimpses into the secret world of childhood.

VI   The Schoolboy

The ruling class in Ancient Egypt were called 'scribes', that is, literates, those who could read and write. This group comprised not only the state officials, but also the higher levels of the clergy, who administered the extensive properties of the temples, as well as a part of the officers' corps.

During the Old and Middle Kingdoms most of the army leaders were civil servants, but when, at the beginning of the Eighteenth Dynasty, Egypt set about conquering her Near Eastern and Southern neighbours and founded an illustrious Empire, the army became the third power in the land, on a par with the bureaucracy and the priests. Among its members the officers of the chariotry were destined to play particularly important rôles. To what extent they were literate is uncertain. The administrative staff, however, who looked after transport and supplies during the campaigns, and the levying and organization of the troops, clearly had to be able to read and write. They also needed some knowledge of arithmetic and mathematics. This category of officers began their career as military 'scribes'. Some of them rose to high positions in the state.

A famous example is Amenhotep, the son of Hapu, under the mid-Eighteenth Dynasty Pharaoh Amenophis III. Originating from the Delta town of Athribis, possibly from a simple family, he became the King's favourite, even replacing his lord at the celebration of the Royal Jubilee in the temple of Soleb in Nubia, and supervising the extensive building activities of this reign. In this capacity he was responsible for the erection of the Colossi of Memnon, in front of his master's funerary temple at Western Thebes, huge statues, over 18 metres high, which dominate the landscape to this day.

So highly valued was the position of literates in society that even the most important officials had statues made of themselves as scribes, squatting on the ground and writing on a papyrus roll stretched on their legs over their kilts (fig. 28). The edge of the roll is held in their left hand, the brush in the right. More than one figure of this type of Amenhotep, son of Hapu has survived. On the other hand, in the reliefs actual writing is always delegated to subordinates, scribes of lower rank, whereas the leading civil servants are merely represented as supervisors.

Some of these even became venerated in later ages, attaining the fame of saints, almost of deities. Best known are Imhotep, the architect of the Step Pyramid at Saqqara, built for his employer King Djoser of the Third Dynasty, and, from the New Kingdom, the Amenhotep just mentioned. Whereas deification in other societies is mainly restricted to warriors and priests, in Egypt the 'wise men', that is, literate bureaucrats attained this position. It clearly shows the exceptionally high appreciation of the Pharaonic culture for writing.

There was yet another category of people for whom literacy was essential, namely the artists, draughtsmen and sculptors. Theirs was the task of converting hieratic texts, written on papyri and ostraca, into hieroglyphs on tomb and temple walls, as well as inscribing them on statues. This would obviously have required a thorough knowledge of both scripts. Although less honoured than the administrators, artists too attained a status above the mass of the population, roughly equal to that of goldsmiths and physicians.

For all these professions a formal schooling was required. Yet, important as they were, we know surprisingly little about the organization of schools and their methods of teaching. The Egyptians in general do not record the means leading to an end, for instance, how they built the pyramids. So they never tell us in detail how boys were educated, nor are there any pictures of schools. The reason for this frustrating paucity of information should be sought in a trait of the Pharaonic civilization. One was interested in what lasted, what was permanent, rather than in the transitory; not in the way something was achieved, but in the end result. To be a scribe was essential, how one became one was hardly worth noting down. Still, as will appear, it is possible, from various sources, to compose a rough picture of schools in Ancient Egypt.

Black granite statue of an anonymous high official in the attitude of a scribe (Saqqara, Fifth Dynasty). (Fig. 28)

During the Old Kingdom no regular schools seem to have existed, except at the court. On a stela from his Fifth Dynasty tomb at Saqqara, now in the British Museum, a certain Ptahshepses relates that after he had "knotted the girdle" (for this expression, see p. 107), he was educated among the royal children in the palace, where "the king valued him above all children". Perhaps he attended a school there. Later on he even married a princess.

It is unclear who coached these princes and favourites of the king. Also to the Fifth Dynasty belongs the autobiography of a "royal prince" called Kaemtjenent which derives from his Saqqara mastaba. He was not only an expedition leader, but also the teacher of another prince. A personage of similar rank may have taught Ptahshepses.

Ordinary schoolmasters are unknown from this period. Usually the boys will have been trained by their fathers, although some elderly men took sons of others as their pupils. In that case they were respectfully called 'father', a custom that persisted through all Egyptian history, so that a man could have two different 'fathers'. The *Instruction of Ptahhotep*, probably from the Fifth Dynasty, distinguishes between "a son by the grace of god" and an actual "offspring who can make trouble" and disobeys his parent. Such an adopted pupil was also called, as a real son, "a staff of old age", one who looked after his elder mentor. Having been instructed "in the sayings of the past", the young man was supposed to be devoted to him who taught him how to behave, for "no one is born wise".

Some wise men took several 'sons'. In the Middle Kingdom *Tales of Wonder* (see p. 4) the magician Djedi had so many students that they had to be transported, together with his 'books', on a special ship. Among fellow pupils of one master a relationship could spring up. Pharaoh Merikare, from the First Intermediate Period, is exhorted by his father in his *Instruction* to be merciful to defeated rebels, particularly: "Do not kill a man whose virtues you know, with whom you have chanted the writings"; that is, with whom you have been at school. In chapter 10 we shall deal with such classmates of the Royal Princes.

It is in the Middle Kingdom that we first come across the Egyptian word for school, literally "house of instruction". It occurs in a text in the tomb of Kheti, a nomarch at Asyut. He urges "every scribe and every scholar . . . who has been to school", when passing his monument, to behave properly and to speak an offering formula for the deceased. Although the text is lacunary, it is possible to deduce from it that scribes were at that time formally educated.

It is not difficult to guess at the reason for the creation of educational institutions in the Middle Kingdom. The state, following the reunification of Egypt under a single, strong ruler, required capable administrators. During the troubles at the end of the Old Kingdom such skills had been largely lost, so that it was impossible to rely any more on the few trained in an informal way by their fathers. It was the needs of the new bureaucracy that occasioned the foundation of schools.

The most important was certainly that in the Residence, which during the Twelfth Dynasty was situated near el-Lisht. It was to that central training institution that the author of the contemporary *Satire of the Trades* brought his son. The first sentence of this text runs: "Beginning of the Instruction made by a man of Sile, whose name was Khety, son of Duauf, for his son called Pepi, as he journeyed south to the Residence, to place him in the school for scribes, among the children of the magistrates, with the élite of the Residence".

It is noteworthy that Khety, who came from the provincial town of Sile at the north-eastern tip of the Delta, bears no title. Probably he was a simple citizen, yet he succeeded in finding a place for his son at the esteemed school for the children of the topmost class, which of course offered excellent opportunities for the pursuit of a successful future career.

Perhaps there still existed a particular educational establishment at the court, specifically for princes and the sons of courtiers. Pepi's school, on the other hand, seems rather intended for the future functionaries in the central government, and evidently accepted boys of lowly birth too. Whether such institutions also occurred in provincial centres is not clear; at least, there seems to have been none near Sile. But it was at the academy in the Residence that the top civil servants were trained, and this may well be the reason why Khety preferred it for his son.

Concerning the age of the schoolboy, the numbers to a class, the curriculum and the didactics, and all related matters, nothing at all is known until the New Kingdom. It is only in that period that our sources begin to flow more abundantly.

As regards the age, education seems normally to have commenced at the same time as in our society. Of course, this was not regulated by law; it will have depended very much upon the physical and mental ripeness of the individual boy, so could have been anything from five to ten years of age. In one case we are at least able to make a reasonable guess as to when the Egyptians first went to school.

The High Priest of Amun at Karnak, Bekenkhons, from the reign of Ramesses II, presents us, on one of his block statues, with detailed information concerning his career. This limestone statue, which is now in Munich (fig. 29), probably provenances from a sanctuary at the back of the Karnak Temple which was dedicated to the deity Amun-Re-Harakhti 'who-hears-petitions', and was built by Bekenkhons himself. The sculpture, as well as its counterpart, now in Cairo, is an unfinished product from the post-Amarna Period, but the inscriptions are due to the later owner. He tells how he passed four years in the primary school, which was situated, according to the text on the Cairo piece, in the Mut Temple at Karnak. Then followed eleven years of apprenticeship in the royal stables, a time during which he learnt the basic ropes of the administration.

Only after those fifteen years of education did his real career in the temple begin. His first four years were spent as a simple priest, still under the supervision of his father who was also connected with the Amun Temple. There followed a progressive rise up the hierarchical ladder, until, after thirty-nine years, he reached the top and served another twenty-seven as High Priest. Altogether, from his earliest schooldays, a time span of eighty-five years. When exactly he first went to school he does not tell us, but he can hardly have been older than five or six. The long-lived Bekenkhons must therefore have been at least ninety when he died.

Other evidence seems to confirm this picture. A Middle Kingdom high official, Ikhernofret, who presents on his stela, now in East Berlin, a report on his management of the Osiris Mysteries at

Limestone block statue of the High Priest of Amun Bekenkhons inscribed with an autobiographical text (Thebes, Nineteenth Dynasty). (Fig. 29)

Abydos, states that he became a courtier when he was twenty-six after having been educated as a foster-child of the king. A certain Antef, from the same period, boasts on his stela, now in Paris, that he received his first office while still a child, that is, shortly after his formal education. Although his age is not mentioned, and we should not rule out the possibility that he may have been a precocious boy, this too suggests an early commencement for schooling.

A final indication can be found in the *Instruction of Any*, from the Eighteenth Dynasty (see p. 15). There we are informed that it is the mother who sends a boy to school, where he is taught to write, hence a primary school. "She kept watching over you daily, with bread and beer in her house". Clearly, the lad still lives at home since she feeds him. Note that, in contrast to Pepi in the *Satire of the Trades* who was brought to school by his father, it is here the mother who takes care of her son's education. "Pay attention to your offspring", says Any, "bring him up as your mother did you".

We also gain from this text the impression that, in the New Kingdom, children generally continued to reside at home during the first part of their studies. Of course this was not applicable when they attended the court school, for then they dwelt in the palace. Nor will Khety's son have lived with his parents, for Sile is far away from the Residence. In such cases the boys were probably placed in boarding-houses, but whether these were attached to the schools we do not know. Hence we should not make the analogy with boarding-schools in the modern sense.

One text conveys the impression that it was not the most sturdy lads who pursued an administrative career. It occurs in one of the so-called *Miscellanies*, anthologies composed by teachers and used as schoolbooks. These comprised various types of short texts such as model letters, hymns to certain gods, praises of the Pharaoh or the Residence, didactic treatises describing the misery of all professions other than that of scribe, etc. The relevant passage contains the following description of a schoolboy:

Be a scribe! Your body will be sleek,
your hand will be soft.
You will not flicker like a flame,

like one whose body is feeble.
For there is no bone of a man in you.
You are tall and thin.
If you lifted a load to carry it, you would stagger,
your feet would drag terribly.
You are lacking in strength;
you are weak in all your limbs, poor in body.

Therefore, "set your sights on being a scribe, a fine profession that suits you".

Although this is written from the viewpoint of the attraction which a military career was apt to exercise on the minds of adventurous young people, about which more will be stated below (see p. 81), these lines show us the delicately-built, less sportive and more scholarly type of boy as the future 'scribe'.

Concerning the school-hours very little is known. In the *Satire of the Trades* we come across the sentence: "If you leave the school when midday is called and go roaming in the streets . . ." (the rest of the sentence is lost), which seems to indicate that, in the Middle Kingdom, the classes were held during the morning. As this text was used as a schoolbook in the New Kingdom, we would expect that the situation had not changed. It may be, however, that there was only a break at midday, and that in the later afternoon, after a siesta during the hottest hours, lessons were resumed.

One of the chapters of a *Miscellany* presents a picture of the everyday goings-on in the classroom. Unfortunately, the papyrus on which it is written is lacunary, but sufficient remains for us to be able to understand what happened. Evidently it is the father who is speaking:

I have placed you at school with the children of the magistrates
— a free quotation from Khety (see p. 71) —
in order to instruct and teach you in this profession with promotion prospects. I will tell you how it goes with a student, when they call him: 'Awake! At your place! Your chums already have their books before them. Lay your hand at your clothes, put your sandals right!'

You have to bring your exercises daily. Be not idle!
They say: 'three plus three . . .'
On another happy occasion you grasp the meaning of a papyrus roll . . . You begin to read a book, you quickly make calculations. Let no sound of your mouth be heard; write with your hand, read with your mouth. Ask from those who know more than you, and don't be weary. Spend no day in idleness, or woe to your body. Try to understand what your teacher wants, listen to his instructions. Be a scribe! 'Here I am', you will say, everytime he calls you.

From this lively description it is possible to deduce certain facts. Firstly, the boys are not only taught reading and writing, but also arithmetic. Reckoning was done silently ("Let no sound of your mouth be heard"), but the Egyptians read aloud. Therefore, the word for 'to read' actually means 'to chant' or 'to recite', as can also be seen from our quotation from the *Instruction of Merikare* (see p. 70). Moreover, we get the impression of a strict discipline, which fits remarks in other *Miscellanies*. In one a pupil states: "I grew up beside you (his master), you smote my back, and so your teaching entered my ear". An almost proverbial expression runs: "A boy's ear is upon his back; he hears when he is beaten". At a later age, when he became an apprentice, even harsher punishments were applied (see pp. 82-83).

We do not know how widely spread the school system was during the New Kingdom. At Thebes there were at least two of these institutions, probably more; one in the Mut Temple, where Bekenkhons received his education, and one at the back of the Ramesseum. It has been generally accepted that there was also a school in or near the Valley of Deir el-Medina, run for the children of the necropolis workmen, several of whom were literate. The exact place where the boys were taught has not (yet?) been located. It seems possible that they went for their primary instruction to one of the temples on the West Bank, for instance, the Ramesseum, and, in the Twentieth Dynasty, the Temple of Medinet Habu. They would have passed their time of apprenticeship with an elderly workman, their father, uncle, neighbour, or whoever. In that period they were introduced into the secrets of drawing and

76

sculpture, but they also continued to extend their knowledge of writing and literature. The ostraca bearing such texts have been found all over the area, in the Valley of the Kings, in the work-men's village itself, and elsewhere. Therefore it seems that this part of the instruction was not bound to a particular place; they simply wrote their exercises wherever they by chance happened to be.

That classes ever assembled within a building is unlikely, even though the word for 'school' is written with the determinative sign for 'house'. At least, nowhere has a structure been excavated that was clearly used as a school. Most Egyptian life took place in the open air, as will have been the case with the classes, the pupils sit-ting cross-legged on the ground around the master or one of his assistants. The phrase 'house of instruction', the equivalent of our 'school', therefore rather indicates the institution.

Perhaps the young children began by writing on wooden tablets covered on both sides with gesso, which played the rôle of the school-slates previously used in our era. A text written with brush and ink on such a medium could easily be wiped out. Several of these tablets have been found, but none with beginners' attempts.

A Twentieth Dynasty piece of limestone, in the shape of a tablet, provenances from Abydos and is now in Brussels (fig. 30).

Pierced lime-stone school-boy's writing board with six horizontal lines of hier-atic text com-prising a letter exchanged between two scribes exhort-ing the scribal profession (Abydos, Twentieth Dynasty). (Fig. 30)

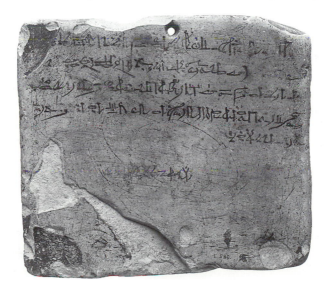

It bears a letter of six lines, in black and red ink, from one priest to another, who was probably his apprentice. The text deals with the manner in which a scribe should behave. It may in fact be a model letter, copied out on the stone after a former text had been erased, although this was done slightly carelessly, as its traces are still visible. Therefore, it may be a school exercise, and, to judge from its contents, not from the primary stage but the product of an advanced pupil.

The tablets have a hole in their upper side, as has this limestone example, through which a cord was passed so that they could easily be carried. Wooden types were also used in the administration, as is demonstrated by a scene from the Eighteenth Dynasty tomb of Djeserkareseneb (TT 38), an official of the Amun Temple at Karnak (fig. 31). He is measuring the corn in a field, which is why he is wearing protective leggings against the prickly ears, and is followed by his son who is also his assistant. As an apprentice, the latter carries a papyrus and a tablet, while the father holds his palette in his hand.

Another writing material used in schools was ostraca. Not papyrus, for that was, although probably not expensive, hard to obtain. It was only delivered by the ateliers to the administration, and even when a palimpsest, used and subsequently cleaned from its initial text, papyrus was too scarce to entrust to young pupils.

The training in writing began with hieratic (see fig. 1). Not, as we do, with single signs, but with words or even sentences. Very few examples of such early exercises survive. We do indeed possess a handful on which single words are written, or even paradigmata, such as: "I am -- he is -- you are", etc., but the script is probably that of a fully fledged scribe, not a beginner. Although these exercises may reflect some insight into grammar, that did not in fact belong to the curriculum.

Instead, the procedure involved the chanting, on a single monotone, of short pericopes from venerated compositions to the boys, who in return would chant them parrot fashion until they knew them by heart. This method is still followed in Egyptian schools, particularly in learning the Koran. When they were familiar with the text, they wrote it down, either from a model supplied by the master, or later, when they had passed the first

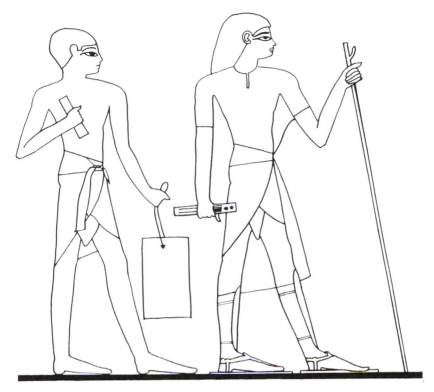

A high official followed by his apprentice son who carries a papyrus roll and a writing tablet (Tomb of Djeserkareseneb (TT 38), Eighteenth Dynasty). (Fig. 31)

stages, from memory. Formerly Egyptologists believed that writing was also produced by taking dictation from the teacher, but a thorough investigation into the nature of the errors has proved that this was not the case, for none appears to be the result of a mishearing.

The order in which the texts were learnt seems to us incredible. One started with the only real schoolbook we know of, the book *Kemit*. This title means something like 'Compendium' or 'Summary'. It is a compilation of polite introductory formulae to letters; a story about the return of a traveller, at the request of his wife, as a model of the narrative style; and short sentences such as frequently occur in ideal autobiographies. All these are in the language and manner of the period when the *Kemit* was composed, that is, the early Middle Kingdom. Therefore in a language the poor students of the New Kingdom scarcely understood, written in old-fashioned hieratic and in vertical columns, an archaism that had, already in the Twelfth Dynasty, been exchanged for horizontal lines (see fig. 1). The pupil's difficulties are comparable to those which the copying of a medieval English manuscript would present to six year olds now! That this was indeed the first exercise that was tackled appears evident from the numerous surviving ostraca with sections of the *Kemit*, several of which are written in an untrained hand. Obviously, it was not the intention that the children should understand what they wrote; they merely learnt a venerated technique.

So it continued. After the *Kemit* the boys memorized and wrote down passages from classical, Middle Egyptian texts, either Instructions or well-known literary compositions such as the *Story of Sinuhe*. Only subsequently did they turn to Late Egyptian texts, from their own period, of which at least the grammar as well as the words were familiar to them. It may be that these subjects were only reached when they were apprentices, and not at primary school any more. All ostraca, and certainly the papyri that bear them, show a well-trained hand.

As we have seen above, the boys not only learnt reading and writing, but also arithmetic. Perhaps singing also belonged to the curriculum. In one *Miscellany* the teacher says to a schoolboy: "You have been taught to sing to the reed-pipe, to chant to the flute, to recite to the lyre". The pupil in this case is certainly beyond the primary school, for he is scolded because he now sits in a brothel among the girls. Therefore, singing seems to have belonged to the secondary stage of his education and perhaps to those courses geared to future members of the clergy - although most vocalists in the temple-choir were in fact women.

Whatever, during the years of apprenticeship the broader education necessary for a particular profession took place: medicine for physicians, cult practices for priests, art for draughtsmen and sculptors, metalwork for jewellers and goldsmiths, etc. We even know of an assistant of a musician and one of an actor, but it is uncertain whether these were actually trainees. It is to this stage that most chapters in the *Miscellanies* refer, particularly to the training of future administrators. Formal higher education as we know it at universities did not exist, and for creative thought there were no opportunities within the bureaucratic system.

Life at school must have appeared dull to many a boy, good only for weaklings (see p. 75). A career in the army, the romance of campaigning in foreign lands, the possibility of drawing the attention of Pharaoh himself by one's gallant deeds, all seemed far more alluring. Therefore, many a chapter in the *Miscellanies* points to the hardships of a soldier's life. There was clearly avid competition between the army and the bureaucracy to recruit the ablest youngsters.

Even in the religious texts included in the schoolbooks we discover a reflection of this tension, for instance in a prayer to Thoth, the god of wisdom and writing:

> Suffer me to relate thy feats in whatever land I may be.
> Then the multitude of men shall say:
> 'How great are the things that Thoth has done!'
> They shall come with their children in order to brand them
>   for thy calling,
> a calling good for the Lord of Victory (i.e., the Pharaoh).
> Happy is he who exercises it.

So, even in a prayer, propaganda is made for the scribal profession. This is also a convenient place to note that there was no regular 'school-god', unlike Nisaba in Sumer. The Ancient Egyptians first promoted Seshat, the goddess of writing, but later Thoth was felt to be sufficient.

Another approach in advertising a scribal career was the painting in deterrent colours of life in other occupations, as we find in the *Satire of the Trades*. It is not for nothing that this became one of the most quoted textbooks. Yet another theme was the picture of a boy, or rather an adolescent, who neglects his studies.

> I am told that you have abandoned writing
> and whirl around in pleasures;
> that you go from street to street,

and it reeks of beer wherever you quit.
Beer drives the people away,
it causes your soul to wander.

- Is not this as if we hear complaints about young people in modern society, although today we expect drugs rather than beer? -

You are like a crooked steering-oar in a boat,
that obeys on neither side,
like a shrine without its god, like a house without bread.
You have been caught out while scrambling over a wall,
after you broke the stocks.
People are running away before you,
for you inflicted wounds upon them . . .
You are sitting in public houses, surrounded by whores;
you sit in front of the girl, drenched in ointment,
a wreath of flowers around your neck,
drumming on your belly.
You stumble and fall flat on your face, smeared with dirt.

Certainly a vivid picture of the tearaway the young man had become. Did it indeed hold them back from following their yearnings? Schoolmasters of all times seem to believe so: "Are you an ass? One will master you. There is no sense in your body".

Evidently, such words had not always an effect, even when the culprit was put in the stocks. On the other hand, these measures do sometimes appear to have brought the lad to his senses, as when a teacher reminisces about his own schooldays, during which he admits to having been full of mischief:

When I was of your age, I spent my time in the stocks;
it was they that tamed my limbs.
They stayed with me three months.
I was imprisoned in the temple,
whilst my parents were in the fields,
and my brothers and sisters as well.

The stocks here mentioned were wooden blocks around the feet, used to hold criminals in prison. Unruly apprentices were therefore treated as lawbreakers. But some succeeded in escaping: the young man of whom we told above, and also another one:

> You set fire to the stocks at night
> that you may climb over a high wall
> in the place where you are.

The last incident was a particularly serious case since the pupil was already thirty years of age, far too old to be indulging in such childish pranks!

On the other hand, the texts teem with remarks about how wonderful a position in the administration could be:

> The scribe is ahead of all work in this world.

> Be a scribe, for he is controller of everyone.
> He who works in writing is not taxed,
> nor has he any dues to pay.

> As for writing, it is profitable to him who knows it,
> more than any other office,
> pleasanter than bread and beer, clothing and ointment.
> It is more precious than a heritage in Egypt,
> than a tomb in the West.

Hence:
> Spend the day writing with your fingers,
> whilst reading by night.
> Befriend the papyrus roll and the palette.
> It pleases more than wine.

The teachers did not shrink from depicting the material advantages of a career in the bureaucracy. One did not have to pay taxes! One chapter in a *Miscellany* describes the beautiful villa and estate that a certain scribe Raia, who was a fairly high official, built for himself. The text enumerates its halls, doors, and portals, its granaries, stables, and fish-ponds, all making it pleasurable to live there. At the end it is duly called "the sustenance of Amun", but that does not sound really convincing.

In the preceding chapter of the same papyrus a pupil promises to construct such an estate for his master, which in a schoolbook seems to us to border on an appalling flattery. Of course, such texts offered an ideal opportunity to teach the pupils, who learnt them by heart, several words and phrases concerning objects and products found at an estate. This was certainly one of the reasons why they were included in the syllabus. That they really stimulated the young man's perseverence in his studies we may doubt. As in the nineteenth century A.D., the Ancient Egyptian schoolmasters firmly believed in the results of moralistic texts. When we fail to do so any more, is it because we have become too cynical?

Not one word has yet been said about physical education. Sports do not seem to have belonged to the normal curriculum (see p. 55) - in contrast to the instruction of Royal Princes and their companions. The description of a pupil as a weakling with soft hands (see pp. 74-75) confirms this. We read in the New Kingdom story of *Truth and Falsehood* that the boy (for his birth, see p. 1) was "sent to school and learnt to write well. He practiced all the arts of war and surpassed his older companions who were at school with him". From those "arts of war" it is clear that he was educated at the court, not among ordinary future administrators.

Were girls also taught to read and write? In the bureaucracy there was no place for them, nor among the clergy, except for a few special posts. Where the feminine form for the word 'scribe' seems, very rarely, to occur, it may in most cases indicate a woman who 'painted', i.e. made-up, her lady.

Yet, there is circumstantial evidence that some women were literate. In a late Twentieth Dynasty letter, written by a man travelling far from home to his son, we read: "You shall see that daughter of Khonsumose and let her make a letter, and send it to me". That the girl's name is not mentioned suggests that she was still young. Although the use of the verb 'make', instead of 'write', seems to mean that she should dictate the message, it does in fact rather point to the opposite.

It has been stated that the palette of Akhenaten's eldest daughter Meritaten, found in Tutankhamun's tomb, shows that she could write. The same would then hold true for a miniature example, of unknown provenance, belonging to her younger sister Meketaten. However, these items bear pigment blocks in several colours, whereas scribes used only black or red ink. They were therefore painting equipment, and as such suitable for the education of Royal Princesses. Tutankhamun's own palette, also found in his tomb, shows signs of having been used. It is indeed proof that he could write, but that was never doubted.

More reliable evidence for female literacy comes from Deir el-Medina. Among the thousands of ostraca there are several which bear letters, mostly concerning trivialities. Some of them are addressed to, or sent by women, a handful even by one woman to another. They deal with feminine matters, for instance, a request for underwear to be made. Therefore, it seems unlikely that both sender and recipient, being illiterate, had to turn to a 'scribe' in order to produce and read the message. Evidently, at least some women in the workmen's families had been to school. In view of the exceptionally high cultural level in the village this does not come as a surprise.

Certainly there existed educated women among the upper classes. In tomb scenes we occasionally see under their chairs, instead of the usual toilet articles such as mirrors, or animals like cats and monkeys, scribal artifacts: a palette, the leather scribal kit bag in which the equipment was kept, and once even a papyrus roll (fig. 32). There is no proof that the lady indeed used these objects, but why else should they be depicted?

For what purpose did such high-born ladies receive a school education? Certainly not in order to obtain a post in the administration. Perhaps to be able to serve in a temple. More probably, however, it was a matter of culture, as in the Middle Ages when noblewomen were sometimes literate, whereas their warrior husbands were not.

Some of the love poems of the New Kingdom, written in a highly artificial language, were put into the mouth of an enamoured girl and may very well have been composed by young ladies. Despite obvious differences, they are reminiscent of the medieval *chansons d'amour*. It would fit our picture of the courtly life style of the period when they were written and were enjoyed not only by women of high society.

As stated above (p. 68), sculptors and draughtsmen were by necessity also literate. Apart from being trained in their artistic profession, they received a formal school education. This is the

The wife of a mayor of Thebes seated beside her husband, with a palette and a scribal kit bag below her chair (Tomb of Kenamun (TT 162), Eighteenth Dynasty). (Fig. 32)

reason why the necropolis workmen who decorated the royal tombs, show such a high level of culture as evidenced by the numerous ostraca with literary texts found in their surroundings.

For the ability of the draughtsmen to write we possess a proof from as early as the Fifth Dynasty. In the pit of a mastaba at Giza a wooden tablet was found, of which, it is true, the board itself was destroyed, but the white plaster coating, with writing in black, red and green pigment, was preserved. The cartouches of King Neferirkare and some names of deities were written in vertical columns, each being repeated four times, except the last one which is written only in triplicate. The pupil seems to have become weary of the repetition! On the reverse are, among other signs, drawings of various species of fish and geese. Since the latter do not function as hieroglyphs, it is evident that the board was the product of a trainee draughtsman.

A different proof occurs on a Deir el-Medina ostracon now in Stockholm (fig. 33). On one side of the limestone flake the master carefully drew, in black and red, the names of King Amenophis I, within cartouches and over gold signs. On the reverse the pupil copied them, in a shaky and uncertain style. He was clearly still a beginner. Note that in the right-hand cartouche the signs drawn by

(a)

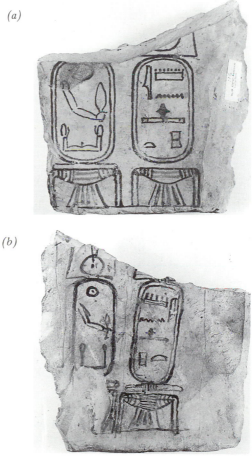

(b)

Limestone ostracon with the names of Amenophis I in cartouches placed over the hieroglyphic sign for gold. (a) The recto written by the master; (b) the verso copied by a pupil (Deir el-Medina, New Kingdom). (Fig. 33)

the pupil have been turned in a different direction, i.e., from right to left.

Other such exercises on ostraca consist of figures, not hieroglyphs, and each is on an individual piece of limestone. A fine drawing of a Pharaoh on his throne, his pet lion beside him, finds its counterpart in a less successful piece by a novice. It is in itself not a bad copy, hence probably from the hand of a slightly advanced apprentice. Both pieces are now in West Berlin.

To work from the very outset of a career belong ostraca with a series of simple signs, for instance the semi-circular ⌣, a basket. To draw and incise a straight half circle was evidently a problem for a boy. Less elementary are pictures of heads and incised hands, or even various hieroglyphic signs such as occur on a piece of sandstone from el-Amarna, now in Oxford. A similar ostracon from Deir el-Medina in the Petrie Museum bears the signs of a human face, a baby, an ibis, a so-called oracular bust, and a hardly identifiable squatting human wearing a large wig (fig. 34). Since some of these are not hieroglyphs, this will also be the exercise of a sculptor's disciple.

Pottery ostracon inscribed in black ink with practice drawings of standard figures by a sculptor's pupil (Deir el-Medina, New Kingdom). (Fig. 34)

88

There is also proof that young draughtsmen copied literary texts when training. A Nineteenth Dynasty ostracon from Deir el-Medina bears a few lines of a literary composition, and concludes with the words: "By the draughtsman Merysakhmet, his beloved apprentice, to the scribe Nefersenut". The 'homework' was dedicated to the master by an advanced pupil.

Although many details still remain obscure, it appears evident from this long chapter that school education is perhaps the best known aspect of growing up in Ancient Egypt. This is quite in accordance with the high appreciation of literacy and the scribal profession.

VII Transition to Adulthood

In many primitive societies there exist mandatory public rituals which mark the transition between childhood and adult life. One possible component, the 'hut-game', is described under the general heading of boys' games (see pp. 63-64). Another element of such a puberty ritual could be circumcision, occurring still in modern Moslem Egypt as will be shown at the end of this chapter.

Whereas there is absolutely no proof that clitoridectomy was performed on girls in Pharaonic Egypt, circumcision certainly existed. However, we possess only one clear representation of the operation. This is the famous depiction in the Sixth Dynasty tomb of the "royal architect" Ankhmahor at Saqqara (fig. 35). In the doorway to room VI there are two adjacent scenes. At the right-hand side, a boy is standing at his ease, with his left hand on the head of a man squatting before him. This man applies something to the boy's penis in order to make the procedure less painful, as is apparent from the accompanying hieroglyphic caption: "I will make it comfortable".

At the left-hand side the boy is firmly grasped by a third person standing behind him, while a *ka*-priest performs the operation. It has been stressed that it was a priest who acts as surgeon, suggesting that circumcision was a religious rite. In fact the title was borne by various members of the personnel of high officials, who were not professional clerics. Therefore, the *ka*-priest could be, for instance, the butcher or the barber of the household.

This 'priest' urges his assistant to "Hold him firmly. Don't let him swoon". In passing it is worth noting that, so far as is visible, the relief indicates that the foreskin was not removed but merely incised with a V-shaped cut. This is confirmed by Old Kingdom statuary. It is of far more significance, however, that in so far as Egyptian wall scenes show particular ages (see p. 26), the boy seems to be from ten to twelve years old, that is, indeed a puber.

90

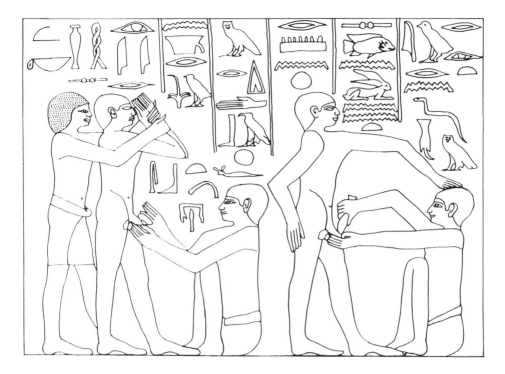

Circumcision scene: right, the preparation; left, the operation itself (Mastaba of Ankhmahor at Saqqara, Sixth Dynasty). (Fig. 35)

It is very probably Ankhmahor who is depicted here, the boy who subsequently became a high state official.

Unfortunately, this is our only scene portraying circumcision as a reality. Indeed, there is one later representation, which occurs in the context of the Eighteenth Dynasty scenes of Divine Birth. It has survived in three copies, namely in the 'Birth Chamber' of the Luxor Temple (fig. 36), in the Middle Colonnade of the Deir el-Bahri Temple of Queen Hatshepsut, and on a loose block from the Mut Temple Enclosure at Karnak. It is regrettable that all three are now mutilated. The former two are extensively damaged and even hard to recognize, the latter bears only the lower parts of the figures, while none of the three is accompanied by hieroglyphic captions.

In all of them two boys (with side-locks), representing the future king and his *ka* ("vital force" or suchlike), are standing, held by two kneeling female figures, while a squatting male person before them performs the operation. From the stance of the boys, which contrasts sharply with the sitting children (as on a lap) with hand to mouth in the other scenes on these walls, it is evident that the royal prince is not a baby any more, although his actual age is uncertain.

However, in this context it is a mythical event which is shown rather than an everyday reality. This is clear from the fact that it is the female Hatshepsut, albeit in male disguise, who appears on the walls at Deir el-Bahri. Since circumcision seems here to have been conceived of as part of the myth concerning the origin of a divine king, it does not imply that in the Eighteenth Dynasty the operation was obligatory for a future Pharaoh. Indeed,

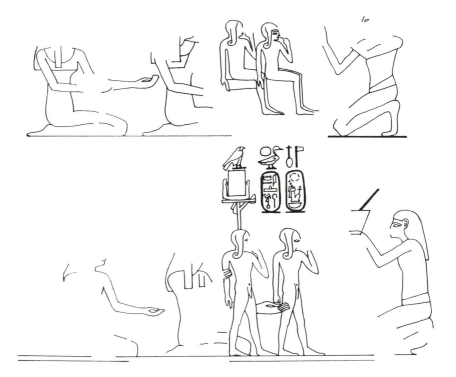

Circumcision of the Divine King and his 'ka' (Luxor Temple, Eighteenth Dynasty (Fig. 36)

92

the birth scenes are probably adapted from early Old Kingdom examples, and hence the circumcision pictures may mean no more than that in earlier times such surgery used to be performed.

Some texts mention circumcision, although it must be admitted that the medical papyri nowhere describe the procedure. Could it be that the operation was not conceived to be a medical action, or is it simply due to the paucity of the surviving sources? Two inscriptions from the First Intermediate Period do seem to indicate that it was still widely practised. In one, on a stela from Naga ed-Deir, a man states: "(when) I was circumcised together with 120 men". This total seems to suggest that an entire age-group was operated upon, at one single ceremony, although of course the object of the ritual was each candidate individually, not the group as a unity. This is on a par with baptism and confirmation in church which may be celebrated for several individuals at the same time. At least, the text indicates that the operation was still very common. In the other inscription, on a block from the tomb of Mereri at Dendera, the tomb-owner relates how he "[buried] its (i.e., the town's or the nome's) old men, I circumcised its youths". It is clear that Mereri is boasting how well he looked after his people, and the sentence suggests that circumcision was a custom undergone by every boy, as every old man should be buried. If our interpretation is correct, the operation appears to have been an element, or perhaps the only rite, of a puberty ritual, constituting the transition from infancy to adulthood.

From the succeeding Middle Kingdom there are three texts which mention circumcision, all of which involve only one boy with no data for his age. Nor is it evident from these instances that many boys, let alone all, had their foreskin removed. As this is a far better documented period, it would suggest that circumcision became less common. The phrase used is: "when I was a boy, before the foreskin was removed for me". It is interesting to note that once, in a New Kingdom copy of an older text, this phrase is written in such a way that one would be inclined to translate it as "before the nappies were removed for me" (see p. 27). The words were not understood any more, possibly because the custom was no longer in vogue.

The Second Intermediate Period has not (yet?) presented us with a single piece of evidence, and from the New Kingdom the operation is recorded in only one instance. Unfortunately, this is a fragmentary papyrus, of which neither the general meaning nor the exact translation is certain. It concerns the later vizier Useramun, uncle and direct predecessor of the well-known vizier Rekhmire. He is described as being received in audience by the boy-king Tuthmosis III, possibly for his promotion to vizier, the highest position in the state. On this occasion, the king asks him: "How many years ago the foreskin [was removed for you]?", to which Useramun replies: "Thirty years ago, oh Pharaoh, my Good Lord". If he had been circumcised as a boy of approximately twelve years, he would be in his early forties, a suitable age for such an exalted office. The Egyptians died younger than in our times, but were also considered adult at an earlier age. Yet, it remains uncertain whether our restoration of the text is indeed correct, and whether, as suggested, the papyrus really deals with Useramun's promotion.

After this Eighteenth Dynasty text there is no written data, except for a remark on the stela of the Twenty-Fifth Dynasty Nubian Pharaoh Piankhy, which is now in Cairo. Four local rulers from the Delta failed to gain audience to the king because they were "uncircumcised and did eat fish". Another ruler, namely Nimlot, that erstwhile vanquished prince of Hermopolis in Middle Egypt, was received, however, because he was "pure and did not eat fish". It is evident that to be circumcised was equated with being pure. This is confirmed by the Greek historian Herodotus who states in his *Histories* of *circa* 450 B.C. that the Egyptians underwent the surgery since they "preferred purity above fresh air". This may be what Herodotus learnt from his Egyptian sources and it seems to have been the common belief in the later ages of Egyptian history.

In the Graeco-Roman Period the priests at least were circumcised, which is in accordance with this concept of purity. However, that cannot be the origin of the custom. Everywhere in the world, and still in the Moslem Egypt of today, circumcision is first and foremost a matter of manhood, including sexuality and fertility. After all it is a form of mutilation, affecting a man's sexual activities.

Other evidence of the habit can be afforded by the mummies. Unfortunately, despite earlier statements, notably by the famous anatomist Elliot Smith who published the first study on the royal mummies at the beginning of this century, it appears to be extremely difficult in the case of human remains to definitely establish the presence or absence of the foreskin. As Elliot Smith's point of departure was his conviction that "all known adult Ancient Egyptian men were circumcised", he was inclined to find traces where others would be more hesitant.

In the Predynastic and Early Dynastic Periods commoners were probably mostly, if not all, circumcised, as attested by the human remains. Evidence from later, royal, mummies is both scarce and indecisive. Indeed, the physicians who investigated the body of Tutankhamun clearly state: "It was not possible to say whether circumcision had been performed". Elliot Smith came to the conclusion that at least Amenophis II and probably also Tuthmosis IV had been operated upon. It seemed to him also certain so far as Ramesses IV and V were concerned. However, recent X-raying in the early 1970s has proved that Ahmosis certainly, and Amenophis I probably, did not undergo the surgery. Elliot Smith also remarks on the odd particularity that a royal child of five to six years was possibly (!) circumcised, whereas another young prince of approximately eleven years, and still wearing the side-lock (see p. 38), was certainly not. The latter is according to our expectations, but the former would be extremely confusing. Taken together, and contrary to what one would anticipate, the evidence from the human remains appears to be most ambiguous.

Some two- and three-dimensional representations should also be taken into account. All Old Kingdom statues which are clear in this respect (fig. 37) show distinct signs of circumcision, as do contemporary reliefs of naked workmen, such as fishermen. Archaic depictions, mainly found on ceremonial slate palettes, likewise display circumcised figures. This suggests that in Prehistory the custom was at least wide-spread, if not universal. It had probably continued to be common during the Old Kingdom. For later times there is hardly any data from sculpture, although naked men are still portrayed, albeit less frequently than previously. Yet, absence of evidence cannot be said to be evidence of absence. Generally

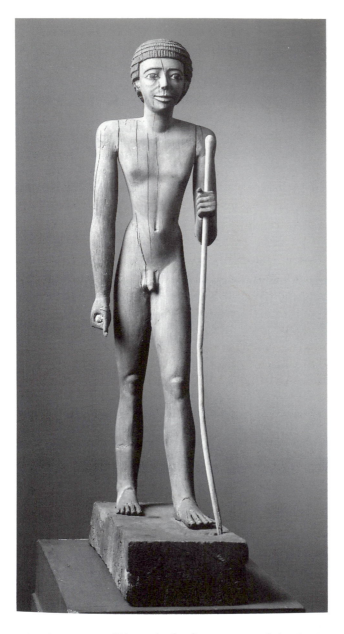

Wooden statue of Meryrehashtef as a young adult, clearly showing circumcision (Tomb 274 at Sedment, Sixth Dynasty). (Fig. 37)

there is not a single case in which a boy wearing a side-lock shows the results of the operation. This implies that circumcision of babies, as is practised by the Jews or the Copts within the birth ritual, was unknown in Ancient Egypt.

To summarize, it is evident that in early ages circumcision was possibly general, obligatory for every youth in order to attain social adulthood. That the phallus hieroglyph is depicted as circumcised constitutes an additional indication. In later periods it became voluntary, compulsory only for particular groups such as boys who were to become priests. Perhaps we may extend the group and suggest that it was mandatory for those lads who were expected to become officials, as the Middle Kingdom examples and the Eighteenth Dynasty text concerning Useramun, if correctly interpreted, would indicate. Indeed, most men of whom statues or texts show that they underwent the surgery, such as Ankhmahor, belonged to the upper levels of society. Yet, one or possibly two Pharaohs were not operated upon, although they descended from rulers. The practice thus seems to have devolved into an inaugural rite rather than forming part of a puberty ritual.

What circumcision can be as an element of a full puberty ritual can be seen from its rôle in modern Moslem Egypt. Here then is a brief description of it as it occurred in the Upper Egyptian village of Silwa, located midway between Kom Ombo and Edfu, early in the 1950s.

The ritual begins with a progression through the village by the initiate, together with his comrades, inviting relations, friends and neighbours to attend the ceremony. On the day itself the guests assemble at the boy's house for a meal. The youth sits on the ground, attired in a girl's headcloth around his neck, and the village barber begins to shave his head, continuing according to the value of the money gifts presented to him by the guests. It is conspicuous that during this action the initiate is addressed as 'bridegroom'. Then, before the actual operation, the lad throws off the girl's kerchief, and clads himself in a white robe covered by a green garment, the typical male attire for religious festival occasions. He is encouraged not to cry, otherwise he will be accused of girlishness.

During the days following the surgery the boy receives special food symbolising fertility, such as boiled eggs, dried peas and salted peanuts. At the end of the period, he is taken on a progress along the houses of the community by his peers, all participants bearing palm-tree branches. In front of each house they chant loudly and require a present in the form of food. With this they return to the house of the initiate where his mother prepares from the gifts a meal for them. It is significant that the food is considered to be the contribution of the women of the community.

The ceremony is full of allusions to sexuality and fertility. An interesting detail in this respect is that during the days after the operation the mother takes her son to the Nile and they throw the foreskin, enclosed in a loaf of bread, into the water. However, there is no direct connection with the physical maturity of the initiate, for the boys are only from three to seven years old. Thus the ritual purely performs a social transition from the asexual world of infancy to the male adult society. Henceforth the boy behaves "as a man"; he shall not weep and wail at a burial as the women do, nor shall he show his genitals to anyone except his own mother, whereas before he could walk around naked. But it is not only infancy that he leaves behind; he is also not exclusively part of his parents' household any more. He is now incorporated into the community as a whole. Therefore, it is essential that the entire village takes part in the events.

Evidently, the circumcision itself is no more than one rite within the ritual. It is not even absolutely necessary, for if the foreskin was congenitally contracted or damaged by disease, the ceremony would still be performed, without the operation. Thus it is the social aspect that is the heart of the matter, not the physical side.

It seems not unlikely that a similar custom existed in Ancient Egypt, at least in early times. Unfortunately, our lack of adequate documentation prevents us from recognizing other possible traces of the *rite de passage*. Although circumcision continued to be performed, there is no proof that in later ages a puberty ritual as it exists in our days was celebrated. It should be stressed that this modern ceremony is entirely due to Arabic influences and not inherited from Pharaonic Egypt.

VIII   Adolescence and Marriage

Adolescence as a stage of social development and experience seems not to have differed from that of childhood, a situation which still pertains in modern Egypt. During this phase the boys and girls of antiquity gradually accepted responsibility for work, whilst at the same time play elements were progressively eliminated. Whether in this process the puberty ritual constituted a definite turning-point is uncertain, the more so since its occurrence is far from certain (see chapter 7).

It has already been noted (see p. 55) that during the Middle Kingdom the age of those engaged in games is not clear any more, whereas in the Old Kingdom the nakedness of boys and girls indicates that they were still children. However, as we acknowledged, the difference may merely be due to the artistic canon. Perhaps the boundaries between children and adolescents were not so sharp. Generally, in so far as they were not part of the training (as for dancers and soldiers), games would have been left to the younger generation, as in our society.

We also demonstrated above   (see pp. 50-54) how, from an early age onwards, boys and girls were introduced into their parents' activities, first by rôle play, and later more seriously. Boys receiving a formal education for the scribal profession were an exception, but they gained acquaintance with their craft in the position of apprentices and assistants (see p. 72 ff.).

These circumstances occasioned a somewhat smooth transition, as far as both activities and behaviour were concerned, from the infant into the teenage world. The exact moment at which one became fully adult is difficult to establish. For 'scribes' it was obviously when they were appointed to their first independent office, yet even then Bekenkhons (see p. 72) was still supervised by his father. For peasants and artisans the end of adolescence may have coincided with their marriage and the start of a family.

Although, as we shall see, this *rite de passage* was less marked than in modern times, it may have been the greatest change in an individual life.

In how far was heredity decisive for a career? Amenhotep, son of Hapu, probably came from a simple family (see p. 67), whereas Bekenkhons (see p. 72), was the son of the Second Prophet of Amun, the highest-but-one position in the Theban hierarchy. Two other higher priests, Hapuseneb and Puyemre, who both functioned under Hatshepsut, were of low descent, as was the great man of that time Senenmut, the main power behind the throne. The sons of these men received lower positions in the clergy, particularly within the royal mortuary temples, doubtless due to their fathers' influence.

On the other hand, three viziers from that period, Ahmose, Useramun (see p. 94) and Rekhmire, were father, son, and the latter's cousin, almost a dynasty. Similarly, in the Eighteenth Dynasty we encounter several families of high officials. Sennefer, the mayor of Thebes under Amenophis II, well-known from his Theban tomb (TT 96) with its impressive grapevine ceiling, was, as will be developed below, the husband of a king's nurse (see p. 146), and, in addition, the brother of a vizier.

Such families can indeed be encountered in every period of Egyptian history, which would seem to contradict the words in the *Instruction of Any*:

> The head of the Treasury has no son,
> the master of the seal has no heir.
> The scribe is chosen for his hand (i.e. his ability),
> his office has no children.

In accordance with this concept many of the upper classes use their autobiographies to stress their competence, suggesting that their progression up the social ladder was due entirely to themselves. As an instance we can quote a certain Mentuhotep, from the early Middle Kingdom, whose stela was discovered by Petrie at Abydos, and is now in Cambridge. He states:

> (I was) one well-disposed and taught by his nature,
> like a child grown up with a father,

100

and yet I had become an orphan.
I acquired cattle, I raised oxen,
I developed my business in goats,
I built a house, I dug a pond - the priest Mentuhotep.

In other words, he became well-off, despite his humble origins, because of his innate abilities. That he really became an orphan is not certain, for the word can also mean 'simple citizen'. This text dates from shortly after the deepest crisis in Egyptian history, the collapse of the Old Kingdom state, in which many of the social values were lost.

This overthrow of the established order became a theme in the contemporary literature. A famous example is the *Admonitions* (also called *Lamentations) of Ipuwer*, which survives on a papyrus now in Leiden. Here we find long sequences of sentences such as:

The poor of the land have become rich,
the man of property is (now) a pauper.

Or: The serf becomes an owner of serfs.

Certainly this is the well-attested motif of a world topsy-turvy, which occurs also in Egyptian literature during the succeeding and flowering epoch of the Middle Kingdom. It has not, therefore, to be taken too literally. Yet, it proves that social climbing was envisaged to be possible, and the case of Mentuhotep aptly demonstrates this idea.

Apart from birth and talent, there was a third factor that determined the career of a young man, namely, the favour he found in Pharaoh's eyes. For the Egyptians themselves this was the decisive element. In their concepts it was the king himself who appointed the officials, civil as well as clerical and military. Middle Kingdom texts on stelae, for instance, bristle with sentences such as:

His Majesty put me at his feet in my youth;

whom the King did know when his nature was still youthful,
    child of the King by his education;

whom the King taught to walk.

Such words were not intended to deny that the person involved should credit his later position either to birth or to ability, or to both. It was certainly these which drew Pharaoh's attention to them. But it was the King who ultimately decided whether the young man should attain a high position.

If, in a particular period, the evidence proves that offices became hereditary, it means that Pharaoh's power was substantially diminished. A clear example of this is found on a Second Intermediate Period stela, found in the Temple of Karnak and now in Cairo. It is the copy of a document by which a mayor of el-Kab transferred his office, which had formerly belonged to his father and his uncle, to a relative of high rank in discharge of a substantial debt. Although the various technical details are not all clear, the function was obviously regarded as his private property, and hence inheritable and even saleable.

This is a proof of what happened in times of disorder when the state did not stand firm any more and no Pharaoh held sway. The ultimate reversal can be witnessed during the Amarna Period, when high officials ascribe their career exclusively to the favour of Akhenaten. So May, one of the top administrators, states in his rock-tomb at el-Amarna:

> I will tell you the favours which the Ruler showed me;
> then you will say: 'How great is what He did for this man' . .
> I was an orphan of father and mother,
> it was the Ruler who built me . . .
> I was without possessions,
> He let me acquire personnel . . . etc.

Was May indeed an orphan in his youth? One may doubt it, as in the case of Mentuhotep quoted above. The assertion rather belongs to the style of that time. Neither did the theme disappear after the eclipse of this particular Pharaoh.

On a stela, now in Leiden, dating from the early Nineteenth Dynasty, a chief sculptor relates:

> I was humble of family, one of small account in his town.
> But the Lord of the Two Lands recognized me,

102

and I was greatly esteemed in his heart . . .
He exalted me above the courtiers,
so that I mingled with the great ones in his palace.

The preponderant position of the king diminished once more during the Third Intermediate Period, and with it we find, from the Twentieth Dynasty onwards, an increasing stress on the noble descent of officials and the inheritability of functions. Indeed, power fell mostly into the hands of a small number of families. Herodotus' words: "When a priest dies his son is established in his place" appear to be virtually correct, although Egypt never developed into a full 'caste' society.

In conclusion, it can be stated that the possibility of making a career depended upon three factors: an adolescent's qualities and diligence, his descent and relations, and, above all, upon the favour of Pharaoh. For the mass of the population an advancement in social rank remained impossible; they simply followed their parents in their profession. A distinct condition for attaining high office remained literacy, with the possible exception of one group: active military officers.

The life of common soldiers is described in harsh tones in the *Miscellanies*, but these were exercises for adolescent 'scribes' intended to divert their minds from the temptations of an easy life in the army (see p. 81). Nevertheless, the picture there presented is not necessarily untrue in all details.

I will let you know the condition of the soldier
in all duties he performs.
He is taken to be a soldier as a child of a pole length
                                        (i.e., *circa* 1 metre)
being shut up in the barracks,
which are divided among the regiments,
with officers over them.
He is confined and goes not abroad
until he becomes a soldier,
struck down with torments.

Or, in another description:

The man is put to be a soldier,
the adolescent to be a recruit;
the child is brought up (merely) to be taken away
    from his mother's bosom.
When he reaches manhood, his bones are scattered.

Evidently, boys were taken into the army at an early age, perhaps when they were approximately ten years old (1 metre tall). That sometimes happened by force (fig. 38). In a letter in a *Miscellany* we read: "The vizier brought three adolescents, saying: 'Place them as priests in the Temple of Merenptah' (at Memphis). But officials seized the men and took them north, saying: 'They shall be soldiers'". Hence, even young temple servants could be conscripted.

We do not know for how many years they had to serve in the army. The early Middle Kingdom *Instruction for Merikare* even suggests a twenty year stretch.

'Raise your youths', says the king to his son,
'and the Residence will love you.
Increase your subjects with new people.
See, your city is full of new growth.
Twenty years the youths indulge their wishes,
(then) the recruits (?) go forth [to the reserves?] ;
veterans (?) return to their children'.

Unfortunately, the translation of these sentences is quite uncertain since the text is corrupt. Yet, the figure of twenty years seems to denote the length of time until the return to civilian life. During that period a soldier could marry, as indicated by a *Miscellany* which states:

His wife and children are in their village,
but he (the soldier) is dead, he has not reached it.

A short term military service for recruits, at the end of adolescence, does not seem to have existed in Ancient Egypt. Soldiering was generally a profession, at least in the New Kingdom.

104

The conscription of recruits for the army (Tomb of Tjanuny (TT 74), Eighteenth Dynasty). (Fig. 38)

Some non-commissioned officers, as might be expected, succeeded in reaching subaltern or even higher ranks, and were able to acquire substantial wealth. An example is Ahmose, son of Ebana, who took part in the campaigns against the Hyksos at the very beginning of the Eighteenth Dynasty. In his autobiography, inscribed on the walls of his rock-tomb at el-Kab, he tells that he was the son of a serviceman, and began his career in a ship's company while still a boy, before he was married. He moved from one vessel to another, and by proving himself a brave warrior he was seven times rewarded, with gold, slaves and fields. Under Tuthmosis I he at last became commander of a naval contingent; not a very high position, but still decisively above the level where he began.

Another successful military man was Amenemhab, by abbreviation called Mahu, the owner of a Theban tomb (TT 85). He followed Tuthmosis III in his Syrian campaigns, captured by his own hand several prisoners, and once saved his master's life on a march near the river Orontes, as he relates in his tomb autobiography:

The King hunted 120 elephants for their tusks. Then I
attacked the largest elephant among them, which charged
against His Majesty, and cut off its hand (trunk), while
it was alive, before the eyes of His Majesty, while I
was standing in the water between two rocks.

All this happened when he still held low ranks, but under Amenophis II he was promoted to 'lieutenant of the army', the highest-but-one military post, and in this function he commanded the royal bodyguard. That he too acquired wealth is clear from his building of an impressive funerary monument.

These persons are nowhere called 'scribe'. Evidently, non-literates did have the chance to progress, although the possibilities for a distinguished career were certainly better when one started as a military administrator. We have already referred to Amenhotep, son of Hapu, the favourite of Amenophis III (see p. 67). Another instance is Anhermose, whose advancement we know of from statues and his tomb at Mesheikh, in Middle Egypt, not far from Abydos.

Anhermose probably originated from Thebes, as did his two successive wives, since they were "chantresses of Amun, King of the Gods". He lived under Ramesses II and his successor Merenptah, and boasts that as a child he already showed his outstanding qualities. He received a school education, but chose a military profession. Like so many, he started out in a ship's contingent, but also served on land.

As a 'scribe' he moved onto the chariotry, the élite corps. He seems also to have been a good linguist, for he acted as "interpreter of every foreign land". So he must have attracted the attention of the Pharaoh, and at a later stage Merenptah appointed him to the position of High Priest of Onuris, the local god of This, in the region of Abydos.

Certainly, Anhermose was not born into a simple family. His father bears the title of 'scribe of the recruits', that is, administrative officer. That he calls himself 'humble' in his youth is a matter of style, as we have seen above. Yet, his autobiography shows that he was a *homo novus* among the higher clergy. In itself the promotion from officer to priest was not unusual; it was an administrative position, as Anhermose himself stresses, for he declares that he looked after the treasury and the granaries of the temple. For a military man this was certainly a rise in social esteem.

To what extent the accident of birth and to what measure talent contributed to a career as an artist is difficult to assess. Among the necropolis workmen living at Deir el-Medina the position of draughtsman, who was mainly responsible for the decoration of a royal tomb, appears to have become a family post during the Twentieth Dynasty. This is also true for the office of 'scribe (that is, administrator) of the tomb'.

Yet, young craftsmen, although chosen from the sons of the members of the crew, had to be appointed by the vizier, Pharaoh's representative, evidently on the recommendation of the leaders of the work-force. In that respect an ostracon from the site, now in Cairo, is of interest, since it enumerates various objects, mostly pieces of furniture, offered to the scribe and two foremen by a father for "the promotion of his son". Together they constitute a considerable value. In our society such a present would smell of bribery; in Egypt it was perfectly acceptable to offer a *bakshish* in such a situation.

Not for all sons of these workmen, however, was there a possibility of succeeding their fathers. Some became soldiers or peasants, disappearing from the community. Whether this was a sheer lack of luck, or depended upon their abilities, we do not know. That those who stayed were generally better off is clear; the workmen were well paid and less harshly treated than soldiers or agricultural labourers, if the descriptions in the *Miscellanies* are to be believed.

It must have been a culmination point in a boy's life when he entered upon his first appointment, even though it was merely a trainee position. In the Old Kingdom, and once in a Middle Kingdom text, this moment is specifically mentioned. In several autobiographies the words "I knotted the girdle" occur, always followed by a reference to the reign of the Pharaoh during which the event took place. It is unfortunate that the age of the participant is never indicated.

The expression points to the so-called 'gala-kilt', the only garment of this period that was worn in conjunction with a linen girdle. It is shown as a distinctive item of dress, with a pleated wrap-over section normally at the right side, on reliefs and statues of several Old Kingdom officials (fig. 39). The phrase is usually followed by the mention of the young man's first office, in one instance by the announcement that he was henceforth educated among the royal children (see p. 70).

Some scholars have taken the phrase "knotting the girdle" to be an indication of a rite within the puberty ritual, but that seems

Painted limestone statue of Ra-maat wearing the gala-kilt with knotted girdle (Giza, early Sixth Dynasty). (Fig. 39)

to be unwarranted. It merely states that the youth clads himself in the ceremonial dress of the civil servants. It is not even clear if it refers to a ceremony, an inauguration ritual, or whether it simply stands as a metaphor for "when I began my career as an official".

From later periods, except for a single Middle Kingdom occurrence of the phrase, nothing is known concerning an inauguration. Hence it is uncertain whether a festival transition was celebrated by which the former schoolboy became an adolescent apprentice.

Probably the start of a married life will have meant a more radical change, since it implied the very end of one's youth. It is therefore even more conspicuous that this passage was not marked by a ritual, i.e. the wedding.

The only indication of such a ceremony occurs in the *Story of Setne* (see p. 3). There it is told how a groom, the son of a general, took his bride, a royal princess, to his house, and according to her narrative "Pharaoh sent me a present of silver and gold, and all Pharaoh's household sent me presents". Then the groom entertains the entire court, after which he goes to bed with his new wife. This at least suggests a wedding as we know it, and as it occurs in modern Moslem Egypt (fig. 40).

However, the story dates from the Graeco-Roman Period. The complete absence of any reference to such a feast in earlier texts or representations seems to indicate that it was rather a late development. There exists no word for 'wedding' in Egyptian, not even in sources such as the love poems where one would expect it to occur. The event is circumscribed as "to establish a household", but that does not imply a ritual. Of the goddess Isis it is once said: "She gives a husband to a widow, a household to a young girl". A married woman is usually called "mistress of the house"; in a few cases "lady of the sitting (i.e. marriage), mistress of the household". Such phrases express the status of 'wife', not the manner in which it came into existence.

For the Egyptians marriage was evidently a social fact, not a legal relationship. It was intended for the generation of offspring, and supposed to be based on a mutual sympathy between the partners. In daily life, pressure, or even arrangement, by parents and other relatives may have been decisive. There is no trace of any religious consecration or sanction.

A bride at her wedding celebrations (Western Thebes, 1989). (Fig. 40)

Let us look for a moment at the so-called *Marriage Stela* of Ramesses II, the modern name of which suggests that we could find in this text some indication for a wedding. The subject was inscribed on several stelae erected at various sites, for instance in front of the Great Temple at Abu Simbel. It contains a description of how, in Ramesses' thirty-fourth regnal year, the Hittite king, following long negotiations, sent his eldest daughter to Egypt, together with rich presents and numerous attendants as a dowry, in order to marry his fellow ruler. Ramesses rejoiced when he heard about "this marvellous event", and ordered an army and several officials to receive the lady properly. He also prayed to the god

110

Seth to end the current spell of very hot summer weather, to which the deity graciously consented. When the princess arrived, the king was exceedingly happy because she turned out to be beautiful. She received an Egyptian name, and was installed in the Royal Palace. But of a wedding ceremony not a single word is mentioned.

As marriage was neither a legal relationship nor confirmed by a religious sanction, divorce, which was purely a private matter, could hardly have constituted a problem. The ideal state of a loving couple depicted in reliefs and statue groups of every era, the wife putting her arm around her husband's waist or shoulder (see fig. 12) does not agree with the facts as extant records present them to us. Of course, such devoted couples did exist, but divorce was far from rare.

From later periods papyrus documents stipulate the property a woman would receive when this happened, just as deeds were also drawn up in view of an impending marriage. Whether these were drafted at some time before, or even after the commencement of a cohabitation is uncertain. Moreover, such documents have not survived from the New Kingdom or earlier. Perhaps oral agreements were then made, and the custom seems to have been that the wife received one-third of the assets acquired during the marriage, whilst she throughout remained the owner of what she had brought in. But even a written record concerning matrimonial property - and that, of course, is not yet a marriage contract - does not seem to have been made. In the case of poorer people it was probably superfluous.

An interesting and unique text in this connection was written on a Deir el-Medina limestone ostracon. In the twenty-third regnal year of Ramesses III, on a particular day, one of the crew called Telmont spoke to the chief workman Khonsu and the scribe Amennakhte, saying: "Let Nekhemmut swear an oath to the Lord that he will not desert my daughter". Then follow the specific words sworn by Nekhemmut: "As Amun lives and the Ruler lives! If I ever will desert in future the daughter of Telmont, I will be liable to a hundred lashes and I will loose all that I have acquired together with her".

111

We do not know at what stage this oath was sworn, whether before, at, or after the beginning of the marriage. However, it is clear that the stipulations are more stringent than was customary; the young man stands to loose all the common possessions. Perhaps Telmont had good reason not to trust the reliability of his son-in-law. He took the trouble to arrange that the afore-mentioned local authorities and two workmen were present to witness this solemn declaration.

Where the only proof of a marriage was its social recognition, it becomes difficult, if not impossible, to differentiate between couples sharing life and a real matrimonial situation. Yet, in some Egyptian texts a word occurs that is usually translated as 'concubine', suggesting that not every cohabitation meant a marriage. In the three cases where we know something about the circumstances, the woman was a second (or later) spouse of the husband, but that does not seem to be indicated by the term.

Other texts distinguish between women who are wives of and those who are 'with' a man. The latter category was common among the lower levels of society during the New Kingdom, and they are the ones who are also called 'concubine'. Some information on this subject can be derived from the legal proceedings of the tomb robberies during the late Twentieth Dynasty. Several women were interrogated, alongside the male accused and witnesses, and their title is sometimes 'concubine', in other cases 'wife'. This may simply be due to the whims of the scribes; it evidently did not make much difference in daily life. Yet, the existence of two terms must refer to some distinction in reality. As it cannot be due, as we would expect, to the fact of whether a wedding had been celebrated or not, it may have depended upon the stability and duration of the relationship, and consequently, on the measure of its social recognition.

One text from Deir el-Medina sheds light on sexual morals among the necropolis workmen. It is a papyrus record, now in the British Museum, of a large number of charges directed against a chief workman called Paneb (fig. 41). He is accused of having gained his job though bribery, of stealing from the workshop and elsewhere, bullying his subordinates, threatening to kill his former tutor and predecessor, and so on. Even if only a portion of it were true, he was a regular scoundrel. Evidently, he was so, for at a certain moment he was removed from his post.

One of the charges runs: "Paneb slept with Mrs. Tuy, when she was the wife of the workman Kenna; he slept with Mrs. Hunero, when she was with Pendua; he slept with Mrs. Hunero, when she was with Hesysunebef". It was one of his sons who uttered these accusations, and the scribe adds to it that Paneb had also slept with Hunero's daughter, and that his son Opakhte (fig. 41), either the accuser or his brother, had done likewise.

Hardly a very savoury picture of life in the village, even if not all has necessarily to be true! It can be noted that Hunero is said first to have been 'with' Pendua, later 'with' Hesysunebef - only Mrs. Tuy is stated to be a 'wife'. From other sources we know that Hunero and her second 'husband' had children, one of them the daughter mentioned in this text. In later years this relationship floundered: Hesysunebef divorced her, an event recorded on a large limestone ostracon now in the Petrie Museum. Whether the affairs between Paneb and the women were contrary to the will or wishes of the latter is unknown. Anyhow, the term used does not mean 'to rape'.

It appears that marriages in the workmen's community were not particularly stable. Hence the fluctuations between the terms 'wife' and 'concubine', or 'living with'. The stelae and tomb walls of Deir el-Medina present only the official picture of loving couples and parents (see cover illustration), the reality may have been different, although we should be careful not to overstress this point. Good marriages did of course occur, as everywhere else in the world, and permanent relationships may have been more frequent than instable ones. The picture conjured up by Paneb's story is exceptional. Reality was somewhere in between this and the rosy image created by the official art.

For our subject, namely the end of adolescence by the foundation of a household, the description of marriage relationships is of importance in so far that the event may be less decisive for the young people's future than it has been in other eras. Perhaps in this respect Pharaonic Egypt most resembles our own days. Never-

113

Limestone stela of Paneb who (above) adores a coiled serpent, doubtless
Mertseger, the goddess of the Theban necropolis; (below) three of his
descendants, including (right) his son Opakhte (Deir el-Medina, Nineteenth
Dynasty). (Fig. 41)

theless, marriage, although without being embarked upon through
a wedding, certainly meant a fundamental transition in life. Soon
the young man would be an expectant father himself, his wife
being pregnant, and thus we have revolved full circle to where our
study began.

114

IX   The Royal Child

Nothing at all is known about the birth or formative years of royal children, apart from some casual references in narratives and myths. In this respect we have already quoted from the *Tale of the Doomed Prince* (see p. 1) and the myth of the king's divine birth (see p. 1). In how far such literary sources contain elements from real events in the palace is not clear. Neither is the scene from the Royal Tomb at el-Amama (see p. 6) very illuminating in this respect.

There is an even more intricate problem: who in Egyptian history are undeniably princes and princesses? Those we encounter in the texts are called 'king's son' or 'king's daughter', but these designations have to be taken literally and were, therefore, not hereditary. Grandchildren of rulers, whom we would also term princes and princesses, were generally not so indicated by the Ancient Egyptians.

On the other hand, from the Old Kingdom onwards we find titular 'king's sons' and 'daughters' who are clearly no offspring of the ruler. The origin of this high social rank is easily explained. In the Archaic Period, power was, in principle, entirely concentrated in the hands of the Pharaoh himself. Where he was unable to exercise it, for instance on expeditions to foreign countries, authority was entrusted to his sons since they were closest to his person. Other offspring who did not occupy central positions in the administration were therefore called 'king's son', while those who represented their father bore only their functionary title since that showed sufficiently that they were princes.

Gradually, with the regime's increased exertion of power over the populace, non-royal officials were appointed. At first the 'king's sons' retained some key posts as overseers of the construction projects of the state, the expeditions, and, above all, the government in general, that is, the function of vizier. During the

Fourth Dynasty these positions too became progressively occupied by commoners, that of the vizier being the last to succumb to the process. Now it was not self-evident any more that such a high functionary was the king's son, and hence it became the custom, if one was indeed so, to include this information in his titulary. So to be entitled 'king's son' was not an indication any more that one was a prince without employment, but, on the contrary, a top bureaucrat.

However, those administrators who did not belong to the royal family also used princely titles, and when, during the Fifth Dynasty, none of them was of royal birth, all 'king's sons' became titulary princes. Above we quoted an example, namely the prince and expedition leader Kaemtjenent who was the teacher of a true prince (see p. 70).

A famous illustration of this development, from the Fourth Dynasty, is Hemiunu, a nephew of Pharaoh Khufu. He possessed an impressive mastaba in the cemetery west of the Great Pyramid at Giza, from where derives his fine limestone seated statue, now in Hildesheim, portraying him as a rather corpulent elderly man. Hemiunu was superintendant of works of his uncle, and in this capacity probably co-responsible for the erection of the Great Pyramid. Moreover, he became the monarch's vizier. In these functions he received the honorary title 'king's son', although as a ruler's grandson he had no legal right to the appellation. According to our criteria, he was indeed a prince, but not so far as the Ancient Egyptians were concerned.

The title 'king's son' is therefore to be compared with that of the European 'Prince', which does not only indicate sons of the ruler - and, in modern society, also further descendants - but is also a rank-title of nobility, as in the cases of the Princes of Orange or the Princes of Monaco.

After the Old Kingdom the use of 'king's son' as an honorary title never completely disappeared from Egyptian history, although its frequency varied. In the Eleventh Dynasty, at the beginning of the Middle Kingdom, we hear of no titulary princes, nor do actual royal princes seem to have played a public rôle in the state. Likewise, 'king's sons' are seldom encountered during the Twelfth Dynasty, except for those crown-princes who became co-regents of their father, and later on sole Pharaoh.

During the Second Intermediate Period, and continuing into the New Kingdom, some local military commanders, as well as leading members of the clergy in some towns, were titulary 'princes'. From the title of one such officer, the 'king's son of Buhen', developed the designation of the Egyptian governor of its African 'colony', the 'king's son of Kush', that is, the Viceroy of Nubia. None of them was ever a real son of the Pharaoh, nor were any of the other military or the religious 'princes'.

The background behind these striking titles is that their holders performed duties directly dependent upon the king. Yet, the same holds true for other top administrators, for instance the vizier, but they are not called any more 'king's son' after the Old Kingdom.

Concerning the real princes of the Middle and New Kingdoms hardly anything has been recorded, except when they themselves became rulers. Only a few others are known to have received governmental positions and by inference political responsibility. It may be, of course, that among those officials who do not mention their father's name a few were actually sons or grandsons of sub-ordinate wives of Pharaoh, but no instance of this possibility seems to have been recorded.

A few king's sons were appointed to the significant post of High Priest of Ptah at Memphis. Among them are: one from the Middle Kingdom, called Amenemhat-ankh, the son of Amenemhat II; one from the Eighteenth Dynasty, namely Dhutimose, probably the eldest son of Amenophis III; and one from the Nineteenth Dynasty, Khaemwese (fig. 42), the fourth son of Ramesses II.

Regarding the latter so much evidence has survived that we are able to ascribe to him not only a career, but also, and this is obviously remarkable, a distinct personality. He clearly represented his father in the second capital of the realm, as did his brother Meryatum at Heliopolis, where he functioned as High Priest of Re. Moreover, Khaemwese, who died in approximately the fifty-fifth regnal year of Ramesses II, seems to have played a leading rôle in the middle period of his father's long reign. Of the many jubilees celebrated by the monarch several were announced by Khaemwese. He built in and around Memphis, for instance additions to the Ptah Temple and in the Serapeum, where he supervised the

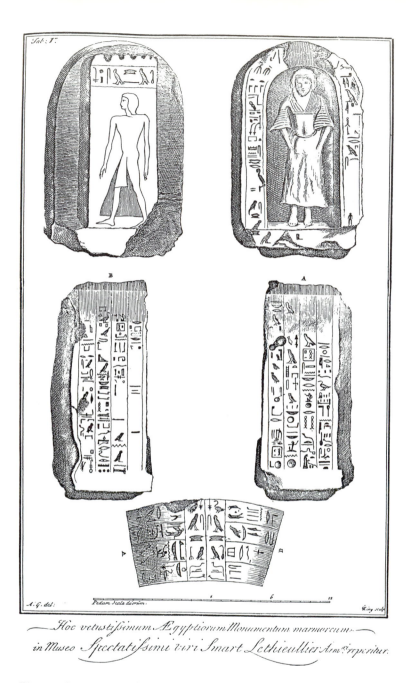

Hoc vetustissimum Ægyptiorum Monumentum marmoreum in Museo Spectatissimi viri Smart Lethieullier Arm.^{ri} reperitur.

Figure of Khaemwese in its naos (Unprovenanced. Now lost, but in the early eighteenth century A.D. housed in a private collection in London). (Fig. 42)

118

burial of more than one Apis bull. Most alluring is his evident sense of history, which entitles him to be called the first egyptologist. He restored monuments in the Memphite area, such as pyramids from the Old Kingdom, recording his activities in boldly engraved hieroglyphs for posterity. One could almost call him head of a department of historic monuments, as well as director of the country's archaeological service. He searched for tomb inscriptions in order to provide the buildings with "name plates/museum labels". Through all these ventures he acquired the fame of a magician, and in later ages he became the hero of the *Story of Setne.* The name Setne is derived from one of Khaemwese's priestly titles, *setem* or *sem.* Whether he was ever the crown-prince is not quite clear. Anyhow, he predeceased his long-lived parent.

Of the other princes cited above as officials far less is known. From Dhutimose we possess a unique monument, now in Cairo, namely a limestone sarcophagus for a court cat. The inscriptions and representations are fully in the traditional style, as if it had been made for a human being: the 'owner' is depicted as a cat, with a scarf around its neck, seated before an offering table, on which, among other food, is a fat duck. Behind it stands a shabti-figure with a cat's head. According to the hieroglyphs the deceased 'lady' was called Tmiao, "The Cat". On the lid of the sarcophagus a text mentions that the receptacle was made by order of the "King's Son and High Priest of Memphis, Dhutimose".

Formerly also the property of the same prince was a whip found among the treasures in Tutankhamun's tomb. Its provenance is not surprising since Dhutimose was an uncle of the boy king.

Of these king's sons, and the few others we ever hear about, all mentions date from the reigns of their fathers. As soon as one of their brothers ascended the throne they drop out of history. In some instances we indeed know that a prince died before his parent: with the high mortality rate a not surprising occurrence. Examples of this are Wadzmose (see fig. 44) and Amenmose, two sons of Tuthmosis I. For the former the father erected a small funerary temple on the Theban West Bank, just south of the spot where the later Pharaoh Ramesses II would build his own mortuary temple, the Ramesseum. The death of both these offspring was the reason why Tuthmosis I was succeeded by the son of a wife of lower rank, the Pharaoh Tuthmosis II.

Another prince predeceasing his father was Amenemhat, eldest son and therefore heir apparent of Tuthmosis III. The same is generally believed of the Dhutimose mentioned above, since not he, but his brother Amenophis IV - who soon began calling himself Akhenaten - succeeded Amenophis III. Yet, in most instances there is no proof at all for the death of princes. They simply vanish. A large number are only mentioned once, and how many never, we cannot begin to guess. Who, for instance, was the boy whose mummy was discovered in the Valley of Deir el-Medina (see p. 38), or that youth who is supposed to be a son of Amenophis II (see p. 38)? What actually happened when one of the brothers seized the crown? That violent struggles sometimes occurred in which several pretenders lost their lives, is more than likely.

Generally, the matter of the succession is not at all clear to us. Were only the sons of a particular Great Queen eligible? In the case of the numerous offspring of Ramesses II that indeed seems to be the case, for, although he reigned into his sixty-seventh year and was over ninety when he died, it is far from certain that all twelve eldest sons were deceased when the thirteenth, Merenptah, succeeded. Perhaps the father's decision played a crucial rôle in these matters. Anyhow, when heirs apparent disappear from the records, it is not certain that they necessarily died a natural death, although the sources themselves remain entirely silent on this point.

As regards the 'king's daughters', their position was different from that of their brothers since, with a few notable exceptions, women never held an office. During the Old Kingdom, parallel with 'king's sons', true princesses as well as titulary ones are in evidence. The latter are either high ranking ladies-in-waiting, or the wives of top bureaucrats. Whether these received the title in their own right, or on account of the standing of their husbands, is not clear.

In later times, whereas honorary princesses hardly seem to occur, genuine daughters of the monarch feature all the more. With them we encounter two fundamental questions: what rôle did they play in the inheritance of the throne, and what should be understood by those, in our eyes, incestuous marriages between Pharaohs and their sisters or daughters?

120

As regards the latter, the only proof for such a relationship is the female epithet "Great Royal Consort". Above we have stressed how difficult it is to define a 'marriage' in daily life in Ancient Egypt, since it was not initiated by a wedding (see pp. 109 ff.). What exactly does it mean if a young royal lady is designated her father's queen? Very probably only that she performed some ceremonies which were specifically reserved for the wife of Pharaoh. Whether a sexual relationship was also involved is highly doubtful, and there exists no proof whatever in an authentic case. The only evidence would be that a child had been the product of such a union, and that seems never to have occurred.

Hence, when one of the Theban *talatat* (that is, small stone blocks from which the temples of Akhenaten were built) shows Nefertiti, offering to the Aten, followed by "the Royal Consort and beloved princess of his [her father's] body Meritaten", we should not conclude that this Pharaoh was married to mother and daughter simultaneously. Moreover, it has been argued that this particular inscription was made when Meritaten was still a toddler, which makes it even less plausible that it refers to a marriage between father and daughter!

Akhenaten's father, Amenophis III, shows in the later years of his reign a clear preference for his daughter Sitamun, who also bears the title "Great Royal Consort". Probably she represented her mother Teye at certain rituals in which the queen had a ceremonial function. That she also shared her father's bed is not likely, whereas an important rôle of Sitamun reflecting the preference of the old king for her above her brother, with all its political repercussions, would be feasible, albeit not proved.

One detail should be mentioned in this respect. If the function of queen was indeed indispensable in the court ceremonies, one would expect that Queen Hatshepsut also had her "Great Royal Consort", just as female mayors in our days have their mayoress. But such a lady does not occur in the records. How the problems in this matter were solved is a mystery. Hatshepsut's daughter Neferure had indeed a function; not that of 'queen' to her mother, but of the "God's Wife of Amun", one of the most important positions a woman of the royal family could occupy during the New Kingdom.

The second question, what was the rôle of women in the royal family in transmitting the right to the throne, that is: whether the princesses were ritual heiresses - even though the actual power remained in the hands of their sons and husbands - is not so easy to answer. Once more almost all our evidence dates from the New Kingdom. One fact is clear: by far not every king's consort was also a king's daughter; several of the Great Queens were children of commoners.

Yet, marriages between a royal son and his sister did occur, for example, between Ahmosis, the first ruler of the Eighteenth Dynasty, and his sister Ahmose-Nofretari. They were both issue of the same couple, whereas in some other instances the royal spouses were half-brother and -sister, as in the case of Tuthmosis II and Hatshepsut. Should such relationships be termed incestuous? The problem is rather complicated. We must at least distinguish between incest, which pertains to sexuality, and exogamy, which relates to conjugal liaisons. Among some peoples where conjugal contacts between particular relatives are strictly prohibited, it may be that sexual relations are even at a premium.

Instead of applying the vague and difficult term 'incest', an attempt should rather be made to understand brother-sister marriages in terms of Egyptian concepts. They have nothing to do with the modern notion of "keeping the blood pure", but such ties are frequent among deities, e.g. the couple Osiris and Isis. Whereas, so far as we know, it did not occur among commoners, at least not officially, a regular marriage between a Pharaoh and his full or half-sister removed him from his subjects and allowed him to approach the divine circle. That may broadly have been the reason for the practice.

During the first years of their life royal children were initially suckled by wet-nurses, and later on looked after by nannies, most of whom were members of the leading families of the realm. Later, during their infancy, they were instructed by male tutors or mentors. Concerning these groups of attendants there exists some information from the New Kingdom, particularly, once again, from the Eighteenth Dynasty. Hardly anything has been recorded from earlier ages.

Several ladies who played rôles in the care of royal offspring are mentioned, and even depicted, in the Theban tombs of that period, for they were the wives or mothers of high officials. They are designated "royal nurse" or "chief royal nurse", sometimes elaborated to "chief nurse of the Lord of the Two Lands" or such-like, with the additional epithet "who suckled the god" (that is, the future king). Evidently, some princes had more than one nurse. In the next chapter we shall see that the husbands and sons of these ladies owed their careers partly to these intimate relationships with the rulers.

In the tomb scenes a royal prince is in some cases portrayed as if he were already king. Of course, these pictures were made subsequently, for it was never quite certain whether a crown-prince would indeed ascend the throne. So, for instance, Amenophis II is seen in the tomb of Kenamun (TT 93) in full regalia, seated on the lap of Amenemopet, Kenamun's mother (fig. 43) - although he apparently was not always the intended heir to the throne. In his right hand he holds, apart from a sceptre, a bundle of strings by which he restrains the bound barbarians placed under his feet. The only indication that the 'king' is in fact an infant is the hand with which the nurse supports his head.

Since Amenemopet is not actually suckling her charge, it is not entirely certain that she was indeed a wet-nurse; she may equally well have been a nanny. That the title 'nurse' in Egyptian is determined by the sign of a female breast is not quite decisive. In another contemporary tomb, that of the military officer Amen-emhab, called Mahu (TT 85; (see p. 105), his wife Baki is shown clearly breast-feeding a king's son. Most intriguing was the scene in yet another Theban tomb, probably from the time of Tuthmosis IV, which is now lost. According to notes and copies of the wall paintings made in the nineteenth century A.D., the wife of the owner was depicted nine times in a row, in each representation sitting on a bed with a child in her arms, some of whom are really being suckled. Probably these babies were members of the royal family.

As stated above (see p. 18), the Egyptian word for 'nurse' is also used, in a masculine form, for male teachers. During the Old and Middle Kingdoms these men were simply styled 'tutor' or 'in-

Kenamun's mother Amenemopet nurses Amenophis II (Tomb of Kenamun (TT 93), Eighteenth Dynasty). (Fig. 43)

124

structor', and not much is known about them. In his tomb at el-Bersheh a certain Iha states: "I was appointed to the post of instructor of the royal children, for I was a man who knows the ceremonial of the palace, one at the top who dares to approach his Lord". Hence it was Iha's acquaintance with court procedures and his personal relations with the ruler - he was also steward of the royal harem - that gained him his post as tutor. Who the princes were that he educated is uncertain; possibly only sons of a nomarch.

From the Eighteenth Dynasty a number of royal tutors are recorded who occupied prominent positions in the state. So, for instance, Paheri, a mayor of el-Kab and Esna, who acted as teacher of Wadzmose, a son of Tuthmosis I (see p. 119), who is shown wearing a side-lock, sitting on his mentor's lap (fig. 44). According to the inscriptions in his rock-tomb Paheri's father, Itruri, was also tutor of this prince, as well as of his brother Amenmose. From the ruins of Wadzmose's funerary temple (see p. 119) derives a stela of a certain Senimose who also claims to have been the boy's pedagogue. The text of this monument dates from regnal year twenty-one of Tuthmosis III, long after Wadzmose's death. It contains the record, unfortunately damaged, of a legal action concerning Senimose's inheritance, so indeed a matter of many years later. Whether Senimose was still alive at the time is not quite certain; anyhow, for our purpose it is only of significance because it records his title. Wadzmose therefore had three tutors; or even four, since yet another of the instructors of Tuthmosis I's children was the vizier Imhotep, whose mummy and funerary equipment, discovered in the Valley of the Queens (QV 46), are now in Turin. As vizier he may have guided the princes in governmental matters, and it is conceivable that this is expressed by his designation "father-nurse of the royal children", a variant of the simple "nurse of the king's son".

The same title is encountered among those of Senenmut, Hatshepsut's favourite and her *éminence grise*, namely 'father-tutor' of her daughter, the Princess Neferure (fig. 45). He will indeed have originally educated the girl, and later on, after Hatshepsut's accession, may have restricted himself in this respect to lessons in politics, while Senimen, the owner of TT 252 and possibly a relat-

Paheri with his pupil Wadzmose on his lap (Tomb of Paheri at el-Kab, Eighteenth Dynasty). (Fig. 44)

126

ion, succeeded him as teacher. To what extent Senenmut's meteoric rise was due to his office of steward of the princess, whose properties must have been extensive since she was the "God's Wife of Amun" of her time (see p. 121), or to the resulting intimacy with the inner court circle, is difficult to establish. It may equally well have been the other way round, in other words, his appointments being the consequence of the confidence which the Queen placed in him.

Black granite statue of Senenmut holding the Princess Neferure. She wears a false beard equating her with the young Theban god Khonsu (Thebes, Eighteenth Dynasty).
(Fig. 45)

Clearly, 'father-nurse' was conceived to be a higher rank than "nurse of the king's son" only. Ahmose-Humai, the father of the Theban mayor Sennefer, was called 'nurse' during his lifetime, but in his tomb (TT 224), postumously, 'father-nurse'.

Yet a more elevated position was indicated by the title 'god's father', in which 'god' means 'Pharaoh'. Physical fathers of the ruler were so designated, although by no means all, as well as fathers-in-law, albeit only rarely. One of the latter is Yuya, with his wife Thuyu the parents of Teye, Amenophis III's 'Great Consort', and therefore afforded internment in the Valley of the Kings (KV 46). Their burial was discovered in 1905, with much of its tomb furniture still intact, treasures that now enrich the Cairo Museum.

That 'god's father' became, towards the end of the Eighteenth Dynasty, a priestly title in various temples, for example in that of Amun at Karnak, is of no importance to us here. It is more significant that it was also a title of tutors of crown-princes. From earlier times, namely the Old Kingdom, only one, slightly dubious instance is known. It concerns the famous wise vizier Ptahhotep of the Sixth Dynasty, the author of the outstanding *Instruction of Ptahhotep*. In its introduction, between other titulary, we find "God's Father, God's Beloved, Eldest Son of the King". The latter is, as we have seen (see pp. 115-116), purely honorific, and whether the first epithet indeed means that Ptahhotep was responsible for the education of a later Pharaoh is quite uncertain.

In the New Kingdom 'god's fathers' as tutors of princes were far from rare. Two of them are Hekareshu and his son Hekaerneheh. The first element of their names, *heka*, that is, 'ruler', suggests that these men were of Nubian descent. In a Theban tomb (TT 226), which has been ascribed to the father, a unique picture occurs of Hekareshu with four princes - all with side-locks - on his knee (fig. 46). In his son's tomb (TT 64) there is another representation of him, now with Tuthmosis IV in full regalia on his lap, similar to the scene in Kenamun's tomb described above (see p. 123). In front of him stands the son, Hekaerneheh, the owner of the sepulchre, with one prince before him and six others, now largely destroyed, following him. There has been much discussion as to who these boys actually are, but one thing is plain: Hekareshu bears the

Hekareshu with four princes on his lap (Theban tomb 226, Eighteenth Dynasty). (Fig. 46)

titles 'god's father' and "nurse of the king's son" because he had coached the future Tuthmosis IV. The son, however, although tutor of at least three royal infants, and possibly even seven, and himself educated in the palace as proved by his title "child of the *kap*" (see chapter 10), is never called 'god's father'. This despite the fact that he was close to Amenophis III, and, particularly, to the Pharaoh's mother, Queen Mutemwia. Perhaps the reason is that when this scene was painted his pupil Amenhotep had not yet become king, even if he indeed was the future King Amenophis III.

One 'god's father' merits extra attention, namely Ay. Apart from being commander of the chariotry - it is conspicuous that many royal tutors bear such military titles - he was the governor of, first, Akhenaten, and later on, of Tutankhamun. Moreover, he was married to Teye, the wet-nurse of Nefertiti (see p. 18). His relations to the royal family were therefore particularly close. When, after the untimely death of Tutankhamun, no suitable royal heir was available any more, the old Ay ascended the throne. He then incorporated the epithet 'god's father' into his cartouche as part of his private name, probably because this stressed his link to the dynasty and constituted his only legitimation.

A special instructor called "father-tutor of a king's son" was Min, mayor of This and High Priest of Onuris under Tuthmosis III, who built for himself a tomb at Thebes (TT 109). There he is once depicted with a prince on his lap, and on the same wall he is teaching Prince Amenhotep (the later King Amenophis II) to shoot (fig. 47a). The caption to this painting runs: "Taking delight in the shooting lesson in the courtyard of the Palace of This [by the King's son Amenhotep]"; the last words have been erased, very probably in the Amarna Period. Obviously, a royal palace existed at This where the prince was staying when Min, a trusted servant of Tuthmosis III, who may have been an officer in his youth, coached him in the noble art of archery. A second caption to the same picture states: "He (that is, Min) gives instruction for a lesson in shooting. He says: 'Draw your bow to your ears . . . . '". The remainder of the text is too mutilated to allow a translation, but the general tenor is clear.

Here we come across an important aspect of the youth of royal princes during the New Kingdom: their sporting activities.

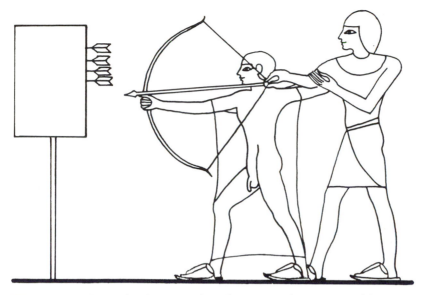

The sportive king: Min gives an archery lesson to Prince Amenophis (Tomb of Min (TT 109), Eighteenth Dynasty). (Fig. 47 (a))

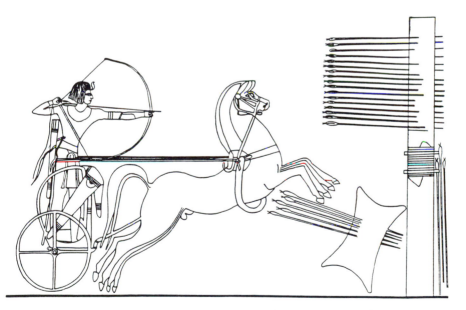

The sportive king: Red granite block showing Amenophis II shooting at a copper target (Karnak, Eighteenth Dynasty). (Fig. 47 (b))

Of course, the Pharaoh had always been presented as a warrior and hunter, such scenes implying that he alone was responsible for destroying evil and protecting and restoring order, or Maat. During the New Kingdom, however, these portrayals were augmented by descriptions of the king's prowess as an athlete.

The representations and texts showing the ruler's or the crown-prince's physical achievements are not realistic; rather they depict a ritual. Self-evidently, the Pharaoh surpasses everyone; his performances, even when exactly described, have not the purport of records. He does not win a game, since by definition he is invincible. As he is the best hunter or warrior, and by that guarantees the universal order, so his physical exercises are a necessary aspect of kingship.

That many scenes of the monarch shooting at targets from his chariot can hardly be realistic is proved by the fact that he is throughout, in battle, the hunt, and at sport, alone on his vehicle (fig. 47b). Normally two people man the chariot, a charioteer and an archer, and we know that the Pharaohs had their own charioteers. Of course, this would not have precluded them from driving the horses themselves, but to have done so at the same time as shooting at the target would in itself be a remarkable performance. On the other hand, Pharaoh's position forbade the representation of another person with him on the vehicle, his queen excepted. In one scene, on a quiver belonging to King Ay, the draughtsman solved the problem of what to do with the reins by depicting them tied around the sovereign's waist; in most representations this detail is simply left unclear.

In itself the motif of a duel, a contest between two opponents, is not unknown in Egypt, where it is encountered in the Horus and Seth legends. Above we discussed the Middle Kingdom wrestling scenes (see p. 57), and in the contemporary famous *Story of Sinuhe* the narrative occurs of a combat between the hero and a Syrian champion, reminiscent of the biblical account of David and Goliath. But with one exception (see below) a Pharaoh is never shown engaged in such a duel. As a reflection of reality it would make no sense, for the king must always be victorious.

Although the pictures and stories of the ruler's athletic accomplishments are ritual, that does not mean that princes were not trained to fit the model. In the New Kingdom at least they were expected to be outstanding warriors, able to shoot and row, to handle horses and a chariot, probably also to swim, which was sometimes necessary during a military campaign. Already from the Middle Kingdom a text, from the tomb of a certain Kheti at Asyut, states: "He (the king) had me instructed in swimming, together with the royal children".

It is particularly of the Pharaoh Amenophis II that in several texts his physical strength and skill in shooting are related. This occurs so frequently and with so many details that one gains the marked impression that it is more than a mere literary motif. On a stone fragment from the Montu Temple at Medamut, not far from Thebes on the East Bank, near the desert edge, we read that Amenophis shot an arrow straight through a copper target, so that more than half its shaft stuck out of the back. Then he challenged his officers to emulate him in a competition, which of course none of them could. The text is lacunary and not always clear, the story probably exaggerated and unrealistic, yet it distinctly suggests that this Pharaoh was extremely strong. Moreover, this is the only allusion to a match between the king and his companions.

On another monument Amenophis' sporting prowess is extensively described. This is the so-called *Sphinx Stela*, one of the most famous inscriptions from the Eighteenth Dynasty. Twice in this laudation it is stated that the Pharaoh had demonstrated his strength while still an adolescent. A translation of the narrative part of the text would seem to be a suitable subject with which to conclude our appraisal of the royal prince. Although, in contrast to the introduction with its formal encomium, the narration itself is not really rhythmic, yet it is written in a genre midway between poetry and prose, sometimes referred to as the "orational style".

Now his Majesty appeared as king,
a fine youth who was well-developed,
having completed eighteen years upon his thighs in strength
(i.e., without having been ill).
He was one who knew all the works of Montu (the war god),
without equal on the battlefield.
He was one who knew horses,

one whose like did not exist in this numerous army.
Not one among them could stretch his bow,
nor could he be approached in running.

After this general introduction describing the prince, a young man of eighteen years, as already an able-bodied athlete, various of his skills are dealt with, the first of which is rowing.

Strong of arms, one who did not tire
when he seized the steering-oar.
As the stroke for two hundred men,
he steered at the stern of his falcon-boat.
One paused after they had covered half a mile
(i.e., *circa* 5 kilometres),
becoming weak, the limbs exhausted, out of breath,
whereas his Majesty was strong under his oar of twenty cubits
in length
(*circa* 10.5 metres).
He paused and landed his falcon-boat
only after he had done three miles of rowing
(over 30 kilometres)
without interrupting his stroke.
Faces were aglow as they saw him do this.

Evidently, the prince was able to handle the large and heavy steering-oar for three miles, whereas the two hundred rowers were exhausted after only half a mile. This is a fair result and looks indeed authentic.

Next comes archery:

He strung three hundred strong bows,
comparing the craftsmanship of their makers,
in order to know the unskilled from the skilled.

These lines are reminiscent of Odysseus' feats on his return to Ithaca!

He also came to do the following,
which is brought to your attention.
Entering his northern garden,

134

he found erected for him four targets of Asiatic copper
of one palm (*circa* 7.5 centimetres) in thickness,
with twenty cubits (*circa* 10.5 metres) between one post and
    the next.
Thereupon his Majesty appeared on a chariot,
like Montu in his might.
He seized his bow,
grabbing four arrows at once.
He drove on northwards
shooting at them like Montu in his panoply,
and his arrows came forth from their back
as he attacked the next post.

It was a deed as had never before been done,
nor heard by report:
shooting an arrow at a target of copper,
so that it came forth from it and dropped to the ground -
except by the king, rich in glory,
whom Amun had made strong,
the King of Upper and Lower Egypt Aäkheperure,
a fighter like Montu.

As here described, it is a dual feat: piercing targets and being able
to hit them all while driving his chariot along them. According to
some representations, such as the fine granite block found as fill in
the Third Pylon at Karnak, and now in the Luxor Museum (fig. 47b),
the targets were oxhide-shaped ingots. They are stated to be three-
quarters of a hand's breadth thick, or, in another text, three palms.
This type of ingot is well-known, particularly from the wreck of a
ship sunk off the southern coast of Asia Minor, near Cape Gelid-
onya, and dated to approximately 1200 B.C. Modern experiments
have proved that it is hardly possible to pierce such targets: the
story, therefore, clearly forms part of the ideology.

    The text continues by expounding on the prince's passion for
horses, the royal animal of the New Kingdom.

When he was still a young prince,
he loved his horses and rejoiced in them.
He was tenacious in working them,

learning their nature,
to be skilled in training them,
understanding their temperament.

There follows an exposition as to how his father, Tuthmosis III, learning about his son's devotion to horses, rejoices at it and soliloquizes:

He will make a Lord of the entire land
whom no one can attack;
eager to excel, he rejoices in victory;
although he is only a charming young man, still without wisdom,
and not yet ripe for the work of Montu (i.e., military campaigns),
he ignores already the thirst of the body,
and loves strength . . . . .

Then his Majesty said to those who were at his side:
'Let him be given the very best horses
from my Majesty's stable at Memphis,
and tell him:
"Look after them, master them
trot them, handle them if they resist you"'.

Subsequently, the prince was ordered to take care of the horses of the king's stable. He did as he was told, and:

Reshep and Astarte (a warlike god and goddess from Asia)
rejoiced over him
as he did all that his heart desired.
He trained horses that were unequalled,
which did not drip sweat in the gallop.
He would yoke them secretly at Memphis
and stopped at the resting-place of Harmakhis (the Great Sphinx).
He spent time there, leading them around it,
and observing the excellence of this resting-place of Khufu and Khafre.

So his trips brought him to the neighbourhood of Giza, where he later on, after succeeding his father - as the narrative states - erected the stela on which this text is inscribed. Indeed the monument was found in the Temple of the Sphinx, now largely destroyed, and there was probably a training course in its vicinity. It leaves us with a vivid picture of the youth who seems to have been the most sporting of all Egyptian princes.

X   The Companions of the Prince

In his *Library of History* the Greek author Diodorus Siculus, of the last century B.C., talks about the companions of an Egyptian prince:

> Now after the birth of Sesoösis (other classical texts refer to him as Sesostris; he is a legendary figure, with some traits derived from Ramesses II), his father did a thing worthy of a great man and a king. Gathering together from all over Egypt the boys who had been born on the same day, and assigning to them nurses and guardians, he prescribed the same training and education for them all, on the theory that those who had been reared in close companionship and had enjoyed the same frank relationship would be most loyal and as fellow-combatants in the wars most brave. He amply provided for their every need and trained the youths by unremitting exercises and hardships.

Diodorus then goes on to recount how they began the day by running 180 *stades* (approximately 30 kilometres) and as a result of their training became a most hardened and robust corps of athletes.

Although written much later, this description contains elements from an Eighteenth Dynasty reality. Indeed, some boys, albeit not necessarily born on the same day, were educated with the royal sons, and trained together with them in the arts of war.

Above we have quoted instances of boys educated at court among the princes: Ptahshepses during the Old Kingdom (see p. 70), and some anonymous pals of King Merikare in the First Intermediate Period (see p. 70). From the Middle Kingdom there was Kheti, the later nomarch of Asyut, who was taught to swim with the royal children (see p. 133), as well as Ikhernofret who is recorded as having been raised as a foster child of the king (see pp. 72-73), which probably implies that he grew up among the princes.

138

During the New Kingdom such companions of the King's sons, educated as pages in the palace, were destined to play influential rôles in the government, as will be seen below.

Very probably these young men received a military training, just as the royal princes did, not only in those sports particularly practised by officers, such as archery and chariot driving, but in all kinds of physical exercises. Conspicuous among the military games were wrestling and stick fighting. Actually, the depictions of these activities seem to present "mock battles", ritual rather than real matches. This is confirmed by the locations in which the 'battles' took place: according to tomb scenes in front of a temple, with the best known representation (fig. 48a) indeed occurring in a temple. It is sculpted under the 'Window of Appearance' in the first court of the Great Temple at Medinet Habu. From this 'window', structurally a wide opening in a wall, the king and his retinue could assist in the events that took place in the courtyard, for instance, the rewarding of valiant warriors and the parade of a victorious army. To the ceremonies there performed belong single-stick fighting contests and wrestling matches, and therefore they are carved in relief under the "royal box". Our illustration (fig. 48a) shows three couples, two wrestling in different stances and one pair single-stick fighting, whilst at the right-hand side the game has ended: the victor raises his arms in triumph, as the disconsolate loser slinks off.

Perhaps the participants in these 'games' were specially trained, not unlike Roman gladiators. In many instances they seem to have been Nubians. The Eighteenth Dynasty tomb of the officer Tjanuni at Thebes (TT 74) depicts a group of such Nubian wrestlers, with the last figure in the row carrying their military standard which shows two contestants grappling with each other. The physique of the soldiers is quite in accordance with the requirements of this sport. That they were also stick fighters is clear from the typical short sticks which they are holding.

The fact that the matches have a ritual character in such representations does not mean that wrestling and stick fighting did not belong to the training programme of army recruits. Moreover, they were practised by boys in the villages, as is still the case in modern Egypt (fig. 48b). The attention displayed in such games by the king and his court at festival occasions, albeit in mock-

Wrestling and single-stick fighting: From the First Court of the Medinet Habu Temple (Twentieth Dynasty). (Fig. 48 (a))

Single-stick fighting: At Abydos (A.D. 1901). (Fig. 48 (b))

fightings, stresses the close relations between the rulers and their soldiers during the New Kingdom.

This keen interest of the monarch in the achievements of his troops is also apparent from an inscription dated to the reign of Taharqa, the great Pharaoh of the Twenty-Fifth Dynasty. It occurs on a limestone stela that was discovered, as recently as 1977, lying face-down along the desert road west of Dahshur. In this text his Majesty relates how he ordered his army to run daily, evidently as part of its fitness training. There follows a harangue by the king to the soldiers in the usual bombastic style.

After this introduction, however, an obviously realistic description is presented of the work-out on a particular day, the date of which was mentioned at the beginning of the text but is now lost. On this occasion, Taharqa himself came "on a horse", that is, driving his chariot - riding on horseback seldom occurred in Egypt - in order to oversee the physical condition of his men. When they started to run, during the cool hours of the night, he himself raced on foot with them for a stretch. After five hours, at the break of dawn, they reached the Faiyum Oasis, having covered no less than fifty kilometres. The soldiers rested here for two hours, after which they returned to the residence at Memphis. The first arrivals were rewarded with food and drink which they were allowed to partake of in the company of the king's bodyguard, while the officers were presented with valuable objects, for: "his Majesty loved the work of arms that was done for him". Clearly, this particular 'manoeuvre' had been a success.

The remark that the sovereign himself joined the runners for some distance seems to be reliable. It shows how he identified himself with the achievements of his army, even taking part in its training. Such a close relationship between the king and his troops, particularly his officers, is found in Egypt from the Eighteenth Dynasty onwards. Above we have mentioned that young men sought a military career since this offered the possibility of catching the Pharaoh's eye during the campaigns (see p. 81). It was especially the companions of the royal prince who could hope for the chance to 'make it'.

Another group of royal companions also owed their careers to a personal bond with the ruler. These were the natural children of the ladies who acted as wet-nurses of the king's sons, the foster-brothers and -sisters of the princes. Several of them remained in close contact with the sovereign throughout their lives. The bond was conceived to be some sort of physical relationship in which milk took the place of blood. Some of these foster-brothers of the monarch attained leading positions in the state. No wonder then that men like Kenamun chose to depict in their tombs their mothers suckling the ruler (see fig. 43).

A similar, although less close, affiliation existed between the Pharaoh and the brothers or husbands of their wet-nurses and between sons of a royal tutor ('nurse') and their sovereign. When, as could happen, these youngsters were also educated together with the princes, such ties became all the more close.

During the Eighteenth Dynasty several members of the upper classes boasted that they were "children of the *kap*". The designation already occurs during the Middle Kingdom, with the variant "one sitting (i.e., living) in the room of the *kap*". The word *kap* here indicates a part of the palace, a school or a nursery or suchlike. Children taken into it became some sort of 'pages' in the medieval sense. It was a position which one was as proud of as the pupils of famous public schools in Britain are accustomed to be, and the title "child of the *kap*" was conceived to be one of the most honourable.

About forty such boys are known from the Eighteenth Dynasty, after which the title seems to have disappeared. Several of them rose to high office, but certainly not all, for some simply continued in the humble profession of their fathers. Others were foreigners, as, for instance, Hekaerneheh, the son of Tuthmosis IV's tutor Hekareshu (see p. 128). Another well-known page was Hekanefer, a local Nubian ruler of Miam (that is, Aniba). He built for himself a tomb in the Egyptian style at Toshka East, south of his city, and he may also be depicted in the Theban tomb of Huy (TT 40), the Viceroy of Nubia under Tutankhamun. Among the African chieftains who bring their tribute to the Pharaoh we see a Hekanefer, the chief of Miam, who flings himself down before his sovereign. However, the common identity of the two is not absolutely certain. As stated above (see p. 128), *heka* is a frequent element in names of foreigners, and so Hekanefer, "The Good Ruler", may have been fairly popular in Miam.

The component *heka* likewise occurs in the second name of a certain Benia, who was also called Pahekamen. He was the owner of a Theban tomb (TT 343), and he too had been a "child of the *kap*". The fact that he was of foreign descent is evident from the non-Egyptian names of both his parents; that he became a fairly well-off civil servant is apparent from his tomb.

142

On account of these and a few other instances it has been suggested that the "children of the *kap*" were, at least in part, those sons of foreign rulers whom the Egyptians transferred to the Nile Valley in order to educate them as loyal servants of Pharaoh. On the death of their fathers they were then installed in their stead. Although this custom doubtless existed, it seems not to be these foreigners who were educated in the "royal nursery". Moreover, most of its pupils were Egyptians, of lower, middle and high rank, and, as we have just mentioned, by far not all later attained high office. Benia, for instance, merely became 'overseer of works', a sort of master builder. Other men who record on their monuments, mostly of a modest nature such as stelae, that they had been in their youth "children of the *kap*", became a draughtsman in the Ptah Temple, a shipbuilder, or even simply a doorkeeper. How highly such persons esteemed their stay at the court's educational establishment is apparent from the frequency with which they record this information. The shipbuilder, Iunena, for instance, does so no less than eleven times in the twelve lines of his stela, now in the British Museum.

Why these humble boys, who remained fairly simple citizens throughout their lives, should have been chosen for the post of 'page' is unknown. The most obvious reason would be their beauty, and that was very probably also the case with their female counterparts who were entitled "Royal Ornaments".

It has been suggested that girls so designated were inhabitants of the royal harem and thus secondary wives of the king, but that appears not to have been the case with the majority. Indeed, they usually seem to have come from simple families, which makes it plausible that they were elected because of their charms. On the other hand, some of the "Royal Ornaments" were daughters of eminent families, while several married high officials. Evidently, as a group they were ladies-in-waiting rather than royal mistresses.

It may be that these are the girls represented in all their naked beauty on the walls of the rooms high up in the Eastern High Gate at the Medinet Habu Temple (fig. 49). The king is here entertained by them, presenting them with jewellery and playing the *senet* board-game with some; he puts his arm around their shoulder or chucks them under the chin. In the past Egyptologists interpreted these portrayals of intimacy as 'naughty' illustrations of harem life. The illusion is partly destroyed, however, by the discovery that at least some of the beauties were Ramesses III's own daughters, for they are once called "the royal children". Moreover, nudity — even the Pharaoh himself is undressed in these scenes, though wearing a crown — had in Egypt different connotations from those in the Western world (see p. 31 f.).

Being a son of or married to a "Royal Ornament" was of significance for the promotion of a functionary. For instance, the mother of the vizier Rekhmire was such a lady-in-waiting, as was also the wife of Ramose, the vizier of Amenophis III. Both viziers are the owners of Theban tombs: TT 100 and 55 (see p. 50) respectively, much visited by the modern tourist. The High Priest of Amun Hapuseneb, under Hatshepsut (see p. 100), was born of such a lady, while the military scribe and later general Tjanuni (TT 74; see p. 139) was married to one. One of the daughters of Menna, a "scribe of the fields" whose tomb (TT 69) is so famous because of its delightful wall paintings (see p. 54), received this rank, as did a daughter of the commander of the marines Nebamun (TT 90), who later in his life was appointed to police captain on the Theban West Bank. It is self-evident that at least some of the royal nurses also became a "Royal Ornament".

The ladies-in-waiting were looked after by the court, certainly until they married. In the tomb of the Theban mayor Sennefer (TT 96) it is stated of one of his daughters, "a Royal Ornament whom he loves, Nefertary", that she was buried by favour of the king with all ceremonies befitting her status. Clearly she died a spinster, perhaps at an early age. Indeed, certain objects found in the Valley of the Queens suggest that some holders of this rank were buried there, amongst the queens and princes. If they were unmarried, the court - that is, officially, the king himself - was responsible for their funeral. In view of the high infant mortality rate this would frequently have been the case, many ladies-in-waiting being still mere children when they died.

In the Egyptian governmental system, in which in theory all power lay in the hands of the Pharaoh, it is not surprising that he surrounded himself with a circle of intimates from his youth.

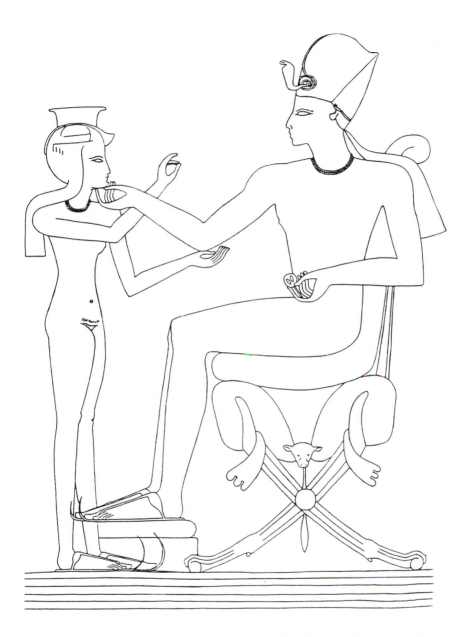

Ramesses III chucks his daughter under her chin (Eastern High Gate of the Medinet Habu Temple, Twentieth Dynasty). (Fig. 49)

These were men with whom he had grown up, whom he knew and could trust: sons and husbands of his wet-nurse, sons of his tutor, sons of the ladies-in-waiting whom he had met as girls in the rooms and corridors of the palace, and especially the "children of the *kap*" amongst whom he had been educated. And then, too, the soldiers whom he had selected and promoted during the campaigns at the beginning of his reign, or the favourite officers of his father, who had looked after and advised him when he was still a crown-prince.

Such a group, in many instances closely knit, can be found at the head of the state under many Pharaohs. A clear illustration is the ruling set under Amenophis II, the sportsman whose achievements as a prince were described in the preceding chapter.

Amenophis succeeded his father, the warrior-king Tuthmosis III, probably after some years of co-regency with him, but still at a relatively early age - he was not the eldest son, for that had been a prince Amenemhat, one of those crown-princes who died before their father (see p. 120). The new Pharaoh inherited the old vizier Rekhmire, who still held office, the third member in succession from one family (see p. 100). After his death Amenophis did not cleave to this line, but chose one of his personal companions, a certain Amenemope, called Payry ('The Comrade'). He was a son of Ahmose-Humay (see p. 128), a steward of the estate of the 'God's Wife' and husband of a "Royal Ornament". Moreover, Ahmose-Humay, the owner of a Theban tomb (TT 224), had been overseer of the harem, and one of Amenophis II's tutors. That Amenemope himself also married a lady-in-waiting is according to what one would expect.

His position was further strengthened by the appointment of his brother Sennefer as mayor of Thebes. Theoretically, the vizier ruled the capital, and only in a few instances during the Eighteenth Dynasty did Thebes have its own special mayor. That this post came under the control of Amenemope's sibling shows the concentration of power in the hands of this family, bolstered still further by Sennefer's second marriage to a royal nurse.

Both brothers built impressive tombs at Thebes: Sennefer TT 96 (see p. 100) and Amenemope TT 29. But their preponderant might is most clearly demonstrated by the fact that the latter certainly, and possibly also the former, were accorded the right to be interred in the Valley of the Kings. Amenemope's last resting place was a shaft (KV 48) south of the path leading to the tomb of Amenophis II, in which fragments of his coffin and clay tablets with his name have been found. Sennefer was perhaps laid to rest in a tomb (KV 42) which had been prepared for Tuthmosis II, who was, however, subsequently buried elsewhere. In this grave some small limestone vases inscribed with the name and titles of Sennefer were found, as well as the canopic jars and a necklace pendant belonging to his wife. Although not decisive evidence, these indications are hard to explain in any other way.

Usually, such figures as a vizier or a Theban mayor remain for us simply names and titles, without any human trait. From the hand of Sennefer there does survive a letter, now in East Berlin, addressed to a tenant farmer and, in so far as we can understand it, dealing with the requisition of various materials. It may not be a private matter, however, but one of the affairs of the Amun Temple at Karnak to which Sennefer was attached during the early stages of his career.

More personal, therefore, is a water-colour palette of polished boxwood that belonged to Amenemope, and is now in New York. It has a narrow compartment for paint brushes in the back and on top eight oval cavities for the much used blocks of dry pigments, in various colours. Clearly, it was intended, and actually utilized, for painting. Amenemope appears to have been one of those statesmen and rulers, like Winston Churchill or Queen Wilhelmina, who passed their leisure hours as amateur painters.

A third administrator of King Amenophis II, besides these two brothers, was the manager of the royal domain Kenamun. He commenced his career as a military officer, accompanying his master on his early campaigns to Syria when Amenophis was still co-regent. Later on he became the steward of one of the king's most important estates, that in Perunefer, the naval-base and royal residence near Memphis. At the end of his life he became the monarch's financial adviser. On the Theban West Bank he built a fine tomb (TT 93), but he may have possessed a second burial place in the North, a few miles south of Giza, for here many wooden shabti figures of him have been found.

Kenamun was a foster-brother of the king, as the picture in his tomb of his mother Amenemopet with the ruler on her lap (see fig. 43) proves. On another wall of his sepulchre some of his relatives are depicted, among whom are Kaemheribsen, who may have been Kenamun's brother or brother-in-law, as well as a mayor of This, whose name is lost. The latter is thought by some scholars to be the archer Min who taught Amenophis to shoot (see p. 130 and figure 47a). Kaemheribsen was the Third Prophet of Amun, hence high in the hierarchy of the Karnak Temple. His ultimate superior was Mery, the High Priest and owner of another Theban tomb (TT 95), who was also the son of a royal nurse, that is, by inference, a foster-brother of the king. His father had been a High Priest of Min at Coptos, so that he belonged by descent to the clergy.

One more man in a prominent position should be mentioned: the Viceroy of Nubia Usersatet. He too served his royal master as a brave soldier during the military campaigns early in the reign, but he was also a "child of the *kap*" as well as the son of a "Royal Ornament". All this implies that he was close to the king from his youth onwards.

These personal relations are clearly revealed in a private letter which Amenophis II sent him when he governed Nubia, a message which Usersatet valued so highly that he had it engraved on a sandstone stela erected in the Nubian fortress of Semna. This inscription is now in Boston (fig. 50). At the top the owner is depicted offering to the king who is seated on his throne, his pet lion beside him. The text, consisting of fourteen lines, is dated to Amenophis' twenty-third regnal year, and stated to be a copy of an order which his Majesty wrote by his own hand "while he was sitting and drinking and making a holiday". Therefore, the tone of the communication is personal and quite informal.

Unfortunately, a large portion of the stela has been broken-off and lost, so that the course of the argument is difficult to follow. It seems that the king warns his viceroy against Nubian magicians and denigrates some Asiatics whom they had once defeated as brothers-in-arms. Evidently, the Pharaoh was sitting back and reminiscing of the happy days of his youth. Towards the end he does seem to proffer some direct advice concerning User-

White sandstone stela of the Viceroy Usersatet (Second cataract fortress of Semna, Eighteenth Dynasty). (Fig. 50)

satet's dealings with his Nubian subjects, but this is tied to what seems to be a proverb, the meaning of which escapes us. Anyhow, Usersatet was obviously greatly pleased to receive this token of trust from his royal master.

Against this background it is surprising that we know of no Theban tomb for Usersatet. Did he build one elsewhere, perhaps at Aswan near his Nubian domain, where he erected many signs of his activities, or perhaps in the North, near Meidum, where he had once been "Overseer of the House" (of the king), apparently a provincial royal seat? It may be so, but appears less likely since all his important contemporaries had their Theban burial places. Moreover, on some of his monuments his names and representations are erased, which suggests that he fell from favour, either under Amenophis II or under his son, Tuthmosis IV.

As stated above (see p. 146), Amenophis inherited some favourite servants of his father. Among them were two prominent military men, Amenemhab called Mahu (see p. 105) and Pekhsukher called Tjenenu. Both were promoted at the end of their careers to "lieutenant of the army" or "of the King"; both possessed finely decorated Theban tombs (Amenemhab TT 85; Pekhsukher TT 88); and both were married to royal nurses. In addition, Amenemhab was a "child of the *kap*"; for Pekhsukher this is unknown. When Amenemhab's wife died, probably at the beginning of Amenophis' reign, she was, as is stated in his tomb, "buried by the favour of the king. One did for her what is done to a noble one".

Alongside these key figures a whole set of minor officials are attested, who were specially bound to the Pharaoh, mostly from his youth on. One of them is the royal butler Maanakhtef, a former "child of the *kap*", later on a court dignitary. There is another butler, Mentiywy, who "followed" Tuthmosis III as a young man and became a good soldier before he officiated in the harem and, later, at court. Perhaps he was a predecessor of Maanakhtef. Another former page is Userhat, who became the "scribe who counts the bread(-rations) in Upper and Lower Egypt", evidently a post in the distribution of food among state officials. He was married to a "Royal Ornament", a rank also granted to one of his daughters.

Among the officers mention can be made of Paser, a troop commander, probably the son of a Nebamun of the same military rank. Educated in the palace as a page, he became chief of the bodyguard of his Majesty "when he was (still) a young prince". Hence he was evidently a member of the inner circle. His Theban tomb (TT 367) was never finished, while his sarcophagus was transported to Sedment in the North and there usurped by a certain Pahemnetjer.

Several more companions of the king from his youth could be cited, for instance Hekaerneheh, the son of Hekareshu, a royal tutor (see pp. 128-130), and himself a mentor of royal princes. But he may have belonged to a later generation.

However, not all mighty officials seem to have been part of this clique. A high personage like Minmose, "director of the great construction projects in the temples of the gods of Upper and Lower Egypt", was probably of low descent and certainly no "child of the *kap*" or the king's foster-brother. Yet he clearly enjoyed a distinguished career. He accompanied the ruler as a military scribe on several campaigns before he became the director of the building activities of the state. That his wife was a lady-in-waiting and his daughter later became a royal nurse, was probably the result of his position, rather than the reason for his success in life. It is characteristic that no Theban tomb is known for him.

Almost all the other companions so far recorded possessed burial places in one particular section of the Theban necropolis, namely the south-west side of the hill called Sheikh Abd el-Qurna. In that area we also find the tomb (TT 97) of another politician who reached the top, without being a member of the select band of the king's companions. This is Amenemhat, a High Priest of Amun, probably the successor of the Mery referred to above (see p. 148).

Amenemhat had an unusual career. As the son of a simple artisan connected with the Amun Temple at Karnak, the "chief cobbler Dhutihotep", he became a common priest in the same sanctuary. He long remained inconspicuous, until suddenly, when he was fifty-four years old, he was promoted to the top post in the Theban clergy, probably jumping over the heads of several of his superiors in the process. For what reason he was chosen for the position of High Priest remains a complete mystery; certainly he nowhere refers to any connection with the royal court. His character seems not to have suffered from this unexpected success, as shown by his autobiography which is inscribed on a wall in the inner room of his tomb. It is cast in the form of a wisdom text:

> He says to his children as instruction:
> 'I say now,
> and let you hear what happened to me since the first day,
> since I came forth from between the thighs of my mother.
> I was a priest, and a "staff of old age" with my father,
> while he was living on earth.
> I went in and out at his command;
> I did not transgress what his mouth uttered . . .
> I did not neglect the orders which he gave me;
> I did not pierce him with many glances,
> but kept my face down when he spoke to me'.

In short, Amenemhat declares himself to have been an ideal son of his father, and by that he creates the impression that he owed his position neither to his relations nor to the special favour of the ruler, but merely to his own humble righteousness and innate wisdom. Whether this is true we cannot prove, but it is obvious that not all the high and mighty of this reign were former companions and brother-in-arms of the crown-prince, although many indeed were.

XI Society's Perceptions of the Younger Generation

In the preceding chapters we have used various English words for young people. Some of them refer to a specific age, such as baby, toddler, schoolboy, teenager, adolescent; others are more vague in this respect: kid, lad/lass, youngster, infant; whilst child and boy/girl cover the entire stretch from birth to adulthood.

In Egyptian there also exists a large number of designations for the younger generation, even more than in modern English, which is not surprising since the texts span longer than three millennia. Many terms spring up and disappear again during the course of the centuries.

However, with a few exceptions the words do not seem to indicate a particular age. One of them, for instance, is derived from the verb "to wean". One would expect it to describe the period of time between the ages of one or two until five or six years, and indeed that does occur. Yet, the High Priest of Amun Bekenkhons (see p. 72) employed it in one of his inscriptions to denote his entire youth up to adulthood, and in other autobiographies it embraces still later stages of life. Thus it is hardly equivalent with our 'weanling'. Evidently, the label became as vague as our 'lad' or 'kid', not referring any more to a specific age.

Some terms for children seem to imply a social rank. An example is the word used during the Old Kingdom for boys after they had "knotted the girdle" (see p. 107), that is, for adolescents who already occupied a social position of some importance. Another expression is restricted to young princes. In the *Sphinx Stela* it is used for Prince Amenhotep when he was eighteen years old (see p. 133), but whether it could also pertain to a lower age group is not clear. It has also been suggested that it bears the connotation 'crown-prince'.

Yet another word for a young person is usually taken to mean 'adolescent', but the ages indicated by it vary considerably.

Bekenkhons applies it to his youth between ten and twenty years of age; Pharaoh Ramesses II was once called so when he was ten years old; King Taharqa when he was twenty, and the Middle Kingdom official Ikhernofret (see pp. 72-74) when he was as much as twenty-six. Clearly, it does not point to a fixed stage in life.

Even the phrase "my child" can present a problem, as does the English expression. Normally in Egyptian it refers to one's genuine son or daughter, but in a few Middle Kingdom and Second Intermediate Period cases it betokens someone who acts as a son, in supplying funerary offerings for a deceased person, although in reality he is no member of the family but a subordinate or servant in the household.

The vagueness in terminology may correspond with the lack of attention displayed by the Ancient Egyptians for the characteristics of childhood. To them an infant was an incomplete adult, still in a state of imperfection.

In the later epochs of Egyptian history, infancy was conceived to be a stage of innocence. On stelae from that period erected for those who had died at an early age, the departed states about him- or herself: "I was an innocent child" or "I was young, one who has not yet faults". In a Demotic wisdom text from the first century A.D., but probably composed in the late Ptolemaic Period, and which survives on a papyrus now in Leiden, we read: "He (i.e. man) spends ten years as a child before he understands death and life. He spends another ten years acquiring the work of instruction by which he will be able to live". That is, only during his adolescence does he reach a level of understanding of life necessary for human existence. This agrees with the words spoken by Tuthmosis III about his son (see p. 136): "He is a charming young man, still without wisdom". And this when Amenhotep was eighteen years old! At that age he was still considered to be "not yet ripe for the work of Montu", i.e. too young for a warrior. Not all societies would agree with this opinion.

We possess at least one text which reveals that the specific nature of a child, as distinct from that of an adult, was not wholly unknown to the Egyptians - although the contents also demonstrate that contemporary society did not want to take it into account. This is the epilogue to the *Instruction of Any*.

154

After Any has delivered all his admonitions to his son Khonsu-hotep, the latter replies that he would indeed wish to be as learned as his father. Then he would act as he is taught. Unfortunately, he is not a sage: "Each man is led by his nature". "The son understands little when he recites the words in the books". Certainly, he has learnt them by heart, but that does not yet mean that he is able to observe their lessons. "A boy does not follow the moral instructions, though the writings are on his tongue".

This Any does not accept. "Rubbish", he says; animals can be trained: "The dog obeys the word and walks behind his master; the monkey carries the stick, though his mother did not carry it; the goose returns from the pond when one comes to shut it in the yard". So why not the boy? To that Khonsuhotep retorts: You do not really listen to me, father. What you state may be excellent, to do it demands virtue. All that Any requires, however, is his son's obedience. He does not really want to listen to his arguments, and compares Khonsuhotep with a crooked stick which the carpenter can straighten so that it becomes a useful staff.

Once more the son complains: "Look, you, my father, are wise and strong of hand. The infant in his mother's arms, his wish is for what nurses him". That is, please, father, take my age into account. The last words of Any, however, continuing the same imagery, run: "When he (the infant) finds his speech, he says: 'Give me bread'".

Such a debate is unique in the pages of Egyptian literature. To our ears it sounds almost modern. The argument of the son is: such an instruction may be ideal but it is too difficult for a boy. In other words: education should make allowances for the age of the pupil. Contrary to these progressive views the father defends the conservative attitude: a boy should obey, if needs be forcibly. In Egyptian society it is the latter standpoint that prevails.

This does not imply that the Egyptians did not care for their children, or did not respect their individual personalities. When we read in the *Admonitions (Lamentations) of Ipuwer* (see p. 101):

> Look, great and small say: 'I wish I were dead'.
> Little children say: 'He should not have made me live!'
> Look, children of nobles are dashed against walls,
> infants are cast out on high ground,

we have to remember that this is a description of a world topsy-turvy. The passage actually states with force that normally parents looked after their offspring well.

Some were even very proud of them, as is apparent from the text on a granite block-statue of a certain Bekenkhons, a priest of Amun from the Twenty-Second Dynasty - to be distinguished from his namesake, the Nineteenth Dynasty High Priest whose autobiography was discussed earlier (see p. 72). The sculpture was made for him by his son "to keep his name alive"; yet, the texts on it are put into the owner's mouth. Concerning the son he says:

> I already loved him when he was still a small boy;
> I acknowledged him as a proper gentleman.
> As a child I found him already mature.
> His breeding was not in accordance with his (young) age.
> His speech was well-chosen.
> There was nothing uncouth in his words.

To our senses this is an overstatement, slightly embarrassing for a son to hear from his father in public. Yet, it was the son himself who had it incised on the statue. In any case, it does show that children could be highly appreciated.

Three-dimensional expression of the care for a child is found in some other block-statues, mostly dating from the Eighteenth Dynasty. In these an infant is shown sitting between the drawn-up knees of its tutor; only its head emerges above the mantle enveloping his lower limbs. This type of statuary occurs particularly in figures of Senenmut with his pupil the Princess Neferure (see p. 125), although sculptures of him in different attitudes also express a similar emotion (see fig. 45).

Certainly, such representations are not meant to be naturalistic, as the beard of the girl in figure 45 undeniably indicates. They evoke an idea in the form of a 'hieroglyph', and should be compared with the ideogram of the breast-feeding mother used in the designation for 'male tutor' (see p. 18), or that of an infant sitting (as on the lap) with the hand to the mouth (see p. 92), the common hieroglyph for 'child'.

156

A further step in this direction is the large grey granite and limestone (the face of the bird) group of Ramesses II and the falcon-god Hurun, discovered at Tanis and now in Cairo (fig. 51). In front of the protecting figure of the bird a baby prince is sitting with drawn-up knees and the index finger of the left hand to its mouth, a sun-disk on its head, and a plant in its left hand. Together these elements should be read as: *Ra* (the sun-disk) + *mes* (the

Grey granite and limestone colossal statue of Ramesses II with the falcon god Hurun (Tanis, Nineteenth Dynasty). (Fig. 51)

child) + *su* (the plant) = *Ramessu* (or, in the Greek form, Ramesses). The representation of the youngster does double service, for it depicts the Pharaoh and, at the same time, stands for the hieroglyph 'child'.

Later on we shall return to the infant in Egyptian art, as one of the means to recognize the concepts concerning childhood. The other avenue of approach is by the way of the texts.

Obviously, children were highly valued and not merely for emotional reasons. Sons in particular were a dire necessity for parents. In the absence of any form of social security, elderly people, if they were not rich, became dependent upon the younger generation. This is expressed by the designation of a son as "the staff of old age", which we encountered above in the autobiography of the High Priest Amenemhat (see pp. 151-152), but which was common throughout the ages. Moreover, it was the son, especially the eldest one, who was expected to build a tomb, or complete it, for his parents, and to look after their burial - also to pay for all this! In addition, after the ceremony he had regularly to bring offerings to the tomb and to there recite the customary prayers.

An expression which occurs frequently in connection with children is "to cause to live" (or: "to keep alive") the name of the father (see p. 156). It does not mean, as we would expect, to keep the family name alive by producing children and grandchildren, but to perpetuate the memory of the deceased by pronouncing his name when passing his monument! It was a duty for everyone who walked along to do so (see p. 71), but particularly for one's offspring. In fact it was of even more importance than the service to the living father as a "staff of old age".

The social need for a son is convincingly expressed in the text on a pottery ostracon from Deir el-Medina, probably dating from the Nineteenth Dynasty, and which is now in East Berlin. It is couched in the form of a polite letter, addressed by the unknown author to a certain Nekhemmut. There were several persons of this name in the workmen's village, and there is no way of knowing which one of them was meant. It is not even certain that a specific person was indeed addressed.

To Nekhemmut.
(May you be) in Life, Prosperity and Health, in the favour of

your august god Amun-Re, King of the Gods, your Lord,
    every day.
What does it mean that you have got yourself into this miser-
    able position,
in which you are now, not letting anyone's word penetrate
    into your ears,
in accordance with your haughty character?
You are no man, for you did not make your wife pregnant,
    as your friend did.
And then, you are excessively rich, but you don't give any-
    thing to anybody.
He who has no children should get for himself some orphan,
to bring him up. Then he will be the one who pours water
    upon his hands,
as a genuine eldest son.

Not a particularly 'nice' letter, but clear in its indication of why
one needs a son in life: "To pour water upon one's hands", very
probably before the meals; and, in a wider sense, to serve the father
whenever he requires.

This rendering of service to one's parents is many times mentioned in autobiographies on the tomb walls. One example belongs
to an early Sixth Dynasty priest in the Temple of the Pyramid of
Teti at Saqqara, who was named Nefersekhemre, in daily speech
Sheshi. His mastaba adjoins that of Ankhmahor (see p. 90), and
contains a description of how well the tomb-owner had behaved
on earth. It runs: "I respected my father, I was kind to my mother,
I have raised their children" (that is, his younger brothers and
sisters). It does not matter whether that was true in this specific
case; it represents the ideal behaviour of a son towards his parents,
the counterpart of care for one's children.

In view of the need for offspring it is evident that childlessness was regarded as a disaster. Particularly for women, but to a
lesser extent also for men, who would have nobody to look after
their burial and supply the offerings. Hence we find the wish for
progeny expressed in various ways. One is the text quoted above
(see p. 7), written on the leg of a Middle Kingdom female figure:
"May there be given birth to your daughter Sah". Another manner
of uttering the desire for descendants is the text on the underside

of certain scarabs. They are inscribed with hieroglyphs that have a different meaning from the normal, so-called cryptograms. The most common sentences run: "Your name may last, children may be granted to you".

Yet another proof for the hankering after issue is encountered in a letter addressed to a dead relative, written on a pot and probably to be dated to the First Intermediate Period. The container is unprovenanced and is now in Chicago. The text, in vertical lines according to the custom of that time (see p. 80), contains a complaint about childlessness. Requests - here: "Cause that there be born to me a healthy male child" - were frequently addressed to deceased members of the family, probably shortly after their demise. Written either on papyrus or on a vessel, they were placed in the tombs. The background is the world-wide belief that the departed has not yet lost all contact with this earth and is still able to help or to harm. No wonder then that one turned to them with a petition for a child!

Although in general both boys and girls alike were wanted in Egypt (see p. 23), it is understandable that the author of this Letter to the Dead particularly begged for a son. The same happened in the text on a stela, now in the British Museum, which dates from the last century B.C. It narrates the autobiography of a certain Taimhotep, the wife of a priest of Ptah, and mentions all kinds of exact dates such as those of her birthday (see p. 15) and of her marriage, when she was fourteen years old. She bore her husband three daughters, but to the grief of them both no son. Therefore they turned to the deified Imhotep (see p. 68) after whom she had been named, and he indeed harkened to their prayers, revealing to the husband in a dream that he should build for him a chapel. The priest did so, of course, and after some time the ardently desired son was born. Unfortunately, only four years later the mother died at merely thirty years of age.

Let us now turn to child representations in two and three dimensions, of which the reader will find a number described and illustrated in this book. In general, the youngsters are depicted as adults-in-miniature. Their age is indicated by their nudity, in many instances of boys by side-locks, and sometimes by the childish gesture of putting a finger to the mouth. This is to be seen rather as a 'hieroglyph' for child than as a picture of a genuine baby or toddler (see also p. 26).

160

If portrayed together with its parents or with just one of them, the child's proportions are not realistic, it being frequently too small. In group statues its head reaches to the seat of the adult's chair, or just above it, to his knee (see fig. 12), and, in other instances, as far as the shoulder of the main figure. It also happens that all the heads in such a group are at the same level, which suggests an abnormally tall infant. In actual fact the size of the body bears no relation with reality, as compared with that of grown-ups. In reliefs too the youngster could reach to the knee or the thigh of his parent (see fig. 18).

If more than one child were depicted, a difference in age between the various siblings is seldom expressed, although the girls are generally more delicately represented than the boys. Rarely does one find traces of the natural plumpness and the proportionally large heads which in reality distinguish the child's body from that of the adult.

This especially holds true for Old Kingdom art, from which numerous portrayals of young people have survived. From the Middle Kingdom three-dimensional figures of children are less frequent. In the Eighteenth Dynasty they again become more numerous, but still show the same general characteristics as in earlier times.

The great break in this respect comes in the Amarna art. Then the artists abandoned the custom of picturing infants in the old symbolic manner by the hieroglyphic ideograph. The Amarna princesses have taken their fingers out of their mouths and behave like real infants by using them instead to point or play. For example, on the altar slab in West Berlin (see pp. 29 and 40) the two groups are brought together dramatically by the linking pose of the eldest princess on her mother's knee who looks up at her as she points to the pair on the opposite side (where the middle daughter is also pointing across). The youngest plays with Nefertiti's hair ornament. The princesses are also not all of the same size any more, so that it is possible to recognize their respective ages (fig. 52, and see fig. 13).

A proof of this more realistic interpretation, here to be seen even in the face, is a very small royal head with a uraeus on the brow. Made of siliceous sandstone, it is now in Hannover. The scholar who published the piece suggests that it is the remains of a

Opaque red moulded glass inlay showing two young Amarna princesses (el-Amarna, Eighteenth Dynasty). (Fig. 52)

sphinx figure, and because he recognized childish traits he felt inclined to identify it as a representation of Tutankhamun. Similar boyish features are displayed on another statuette of this Pharaoh, in petrified wood, and now in Cairo. Of somewhat riper years is the face emerging from the blue lotus-flower. Sculpted in painted wood this beautiful object was found in the boy king's tomb.

162

Even if the suggestions that these countenances exhibit child-ish characteristics are, in each separate case, debatable, taken together they show that the Amarna Period constitutes a new development in the portrayal of infants. This corresponds with a vividness in some contemporaneous Theban tomb scenes, for instance those of Neferhotep (TT 49; see fig. 22). And, although Nineteenth Dynasty art mainly returned to the old principles, the children on our cover illustration display a greater naturalness than those in Old Kingdom tombs (see, for instance, fig. 18).

Yet, realistic details were never completely absent from Egyptian art. In the Fifth Dynasty mastaba of Nefer and Kahay (see p. 42) there is the scene of a woman sitting at the entrance to a bower and watching dancing girls. Before her stands her little daughter, dressed in a long gown and looking up at her - evidently she was not particularly enthralled by the performance! With her left hand she just touches her mother's hand which rests on the lap: a rare display of tenderness.

Such details are fairly scarce, and far dispersed. Infants are mostly merely pictured as a type, and that a small adult. "The child in Egyptian art" is hardly to be viewed as an interesting subject within the field of art history, and it is not surprising that such a study has never been written.

This agrees with the Egyptians' concepts of childhood in general. Although well aware of the individuality of each youngster, as a stage in life youth was conceived to be "not-yet-adulthood", with full stress on the "not yet". As a necessary transitory stage, without its own value, the aim was simply to prepare the child for the future as quickly as possible, without seeking to promote his own innate possibilities. Growing up in Ancient Egypt was thus still far removed from "The Age of the Child".

Nevertheless, offspring were valued, and we can aptly conclude our study with the words of the oft-quoted Any in his *Instructions:*

Happy is the man whose people are many;
He is saluted on account of his progeny.

———————•••©>©©©©©©•••—————

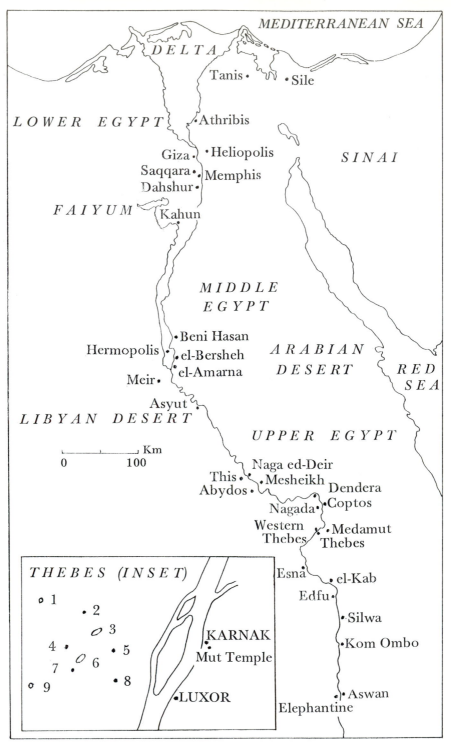

MEDITERRANEAN SEA

DELTA

Tanis •   • Sile

LOWER EGYPT   •Athribis

SINAI

Giza •   • Heliopolis
Saqqara • • Memphis
Dahshur •

FAIYUM   •Kahun

MIDDLE
EGYPT

•Beni Hasan
Hermopolis • •el-Bersheh
        •el-Amarna

ARABIAN
DESERT

RED
SEA

Meir •

Asyut •

LIBYAN DESERT

UPPER EGYPT

Km
0   100

Naga ed-Deir
This • •Mesheikh
Abydos •   Dendera
        •Coptos
Nagada •
Western   •Medamut
Thebes   Thebes

Esna •
        • el-Kab

Edfu •

•Silwa

•Kom Ombo

THEBES (INSET)

∘ 1
    • 2
      ∘ 3
4 •   • 5
7   ∘ 6
∘ 9   • 8

KARNAK
Mut Temple

•LUXOR

• Aswan
Elephantine

Key to inset of Thebes: 1. Valley of the Kings; 2. Deir el-Bahri; 3. Sheikh Abd el-Qurna; 4. Deir el-Medina; 5. Ramesseum; 6. Qurnet Murai; 7. Medinet Habu; 8. Colossi of Memnon; 9. Valley of the Queens.

Map of Egypt, showing the sites mentioned in the text and the captions (Fig. 53)

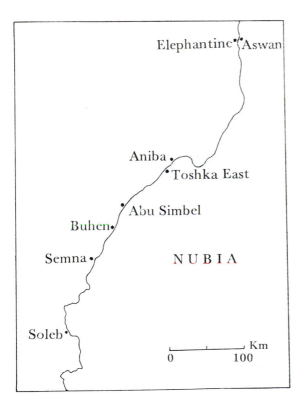

List of Museums

(mentioned in the text under toponyms)

Berlin (East)	:	Staatliche Museen zu Berlin. Ägyptisches Museum.
Berlin (West)	:	Staatliche Museen Preussischer Kulturbesitz. Ägyptisches Museum.
Bologna	:	Museo Civico.
Bolton	:	Central Museum and Art Gallery.
Boston	:	Museum of Fine Arts.
Brussels	:	Musées Royaux d'Art et d'Histoire.
Cairo	:	Egyptian Museum/Musée Egyptien.
Cambridge	:	Fitzwilliam Museum.
Chicago	:	Oriental Institute.
Hannover	:	Kestner Museum.
Hildesheim	:	Pelizaeus-Museum.
Leiden	:	Rijksmuseum van Oudheden.
Manchester	:	Manchester Museum, University of Manchester.
New York	:	Metropolitan Museum of Art.
Oxford	:	Ashmolean Museum.
Paris	:	Musée du Louvre.
Stockholm	:	Medelhavsmuseet.
Toulouse	:	Musée Georges Labit.
Tubingen	:	Ägyptische Sammlung der Universität Tübingen.
Turin	:	Museo Egizio.

Select Bibliography

I - *General*

Lexikon der Ägyptologie. Begründet von Wolfgang Helck und Eberhard Otto, 6 vols., Wiesbaden, 1972-1986.

Brunner-Traut, Emma, *Die Alten Ägypter*. Verborgenes Leben unter Pharaonen, Stuttgart, 1974 (especially chapter 3: 'Familienzuwachs').

Unger, Reinhart, *Die Mutter mit dem Kinde*. Inauguraldissertation Leipzig, 1957.

II - *Special Subjects*

Baines, John, Egyptian Twins, *Orientalia* 54 (1985), 461-482.

Brunner, Hellmut, *Altägyptische Erziehung*, Wiesbaden, 1957.

Brunner-Traut, Emma, Gravidenflasche. Das Salben des Mutterleibes, *in: Archäologie und Altes Testament*. Festschrift für Kurt Galling. Herausgegeben von A. Kuschke und E. Kutsch, Tübingen, 1970, 35-48.

Brunner-Traut, Emma, Das Muttermilchkrüglein. Ammen mit Stillumhang und Mondamulett, *Die Welt des Orients* 5 (1969-1970), 145-164.

Brunner-Traut, Emma, Die Wochenlaube, *Mitteilungen des Instituts für Orientforschung 3* (1955), 11-30.

Cole, Dorothea, Obstetrics for Women in Ancient Egypt, *Discussions in Egyptology* 5 (1986), 27-33.

David, A.R., Toys and Games in the Manchester Museum Collection, *in: Glimpses of Ancient Egypt*. Studies in Honour of H.W. Fairman. Edited by John Ruffle, G.A. Gaballa and Kenneth A. Kitchen, Warminster, 1979, 12-15.

Decker, Wolfgang, *Sport und Spiel im Alten Ägypten*, München, 1987.

Erman, A., *Zaubersprüche für Mutter und Kind*. Aus dem Papyrus 3027 des Berliner Museums = Abh. Kön. Preuss. Akad. der Wiss. zu Berlin, Phil.-hist. Klasse 1901, 1-52; reprinted in: Adolf Erman, *Akademieschriften*, Leipzig, 1986, I, 455-504.

Feucht, Erika, The ḥrdw n k3p Reconsidered, *in: Pharaonic Egypt. The Bible and Christianity*. Edited by Sarah Israelit-Groll, Jerusalem, 1985, 38-47.

Feucht, Erika, Gattenwahl, Ehe und Nachkommenschaft im alten Ägypten, *in: Geschlechtsreife und Legitimation zur Zeugung*. Herausgegeben von E.W. Müller, Freiburg/München, 1985, 55-84.

Feucht, Erika, Geburt, Kindheit, Jugend und Ausbildung im Alten Ägypten, *in: Zur Sozialgeschichte der Kindheit*. Herausgegeben von J. Martin und A. Nitschke, Freiburg/München, 1986, 225-265.

Fischer-Elfert, Hans-Werner, Der Schreiber als Lehrer in der frühen ägyptischen Hochkultur, *in: Schreiber, Magister, Lehrer*. Zur Geschichte und Funktion eines Berufsstandes. Herausgegeben von Johann Georg Prinz von Hohenzollern und Max Liedtke, Bad Heilbrunn, 1989, 60-70.

Jonckheere, Fr., La circoncision des anciens Egyptiens, *Centaurus* 1 (1951), 212-234.

Manuelian, Peter Der, *Studies in the Reign of Amenophis II* (= Hildesheimer Ägyptologische Beiträge, 26), Hildesheim, 1987.

Pinch, Geraldine, Childbirth and Female Figurines at Deir el-Medina and el-'Amarna, *Orientalia* 52 (1983), 405-414.

Schmitz, Bettina, *Untersuchungen zum Titel s3-njśwt "Königssohn"* (= Habelts Dissertationsdrucke. Reihe Ägyptologie, 2), Bonn, 1976.

Théodoridès, Aristide, L'enfant dans les institutions pharaoniques, in: *L'Enfant dans les civilisations orientales. Het kind in de oosterse beschavingen*. Onder leiding van/sous la direction de A. Théodoridès, P. Naster, J. Ries, Leuven, 1980 (= Acta Orientalia Belgica, 2), 89-102.

Touny, A.D. - Steffen Wenig, *Die Sport im Alten Ägypten*, Leipzig, 1969.

Walle, B. van de, *La transmission des textes littéraires égyptiens*, Bruxelles, 1948.

Wit, Constant de, La circoncision chez les anciens Egyptiens, *Zeitschrift für ägyptische Sprache und Altertumskunde* 99 (1972), 41-48.

170

List of Tombs at Thebes

Page numbers in italic refer to illustrations

The following abbreviations occur in the text, and precede the official number assigned to a particular tomb in the Theban necropolis by the Antiquities Service. The numbering follows no topographical order.

TT   =   Theban Tomb (private)

KV   =   (tomb in the) Valley of the Kings

QV   =   (tomb in the) Valley of the Queens

Index

Page numbers in italic refer to illustrations